POWER BAROMETER

Library of Congress Control Number: 2023944593

ISBN (paperback): 978-1-956450-85-9
ISBN (Ebook): 978-1-956450-86-6

ARMINLEAR

Armin Lear Press, Inc.
215 W Riverside Drive, #4362
Estes Park, CO 80517

POWER BAROMETER

HOW TO MANAGE
PERSONAL ENERGY
FOR BUSINESS SUCCESS

JOSEFINE CAMPBELL

PRAISE FOR POWER BAROMETER

"In this book, Josefine Campbell focuses on the essence of being a good leader—how can we become a better version of ourselves? The combination of optimizing energy and mental presence is a powerful message that many leaders will be able to use to become a better version of themselves. At a turning point in my life, I realized what it can do to [help me] be mentally agile. After that, it helped me handle my work with Pandora's IPO. Today I use it in my work in Carlsberg, but also privately. In my opinion, it is more a self-development book than a management book because you can use the tools in all aspects of life."

—JESPER SABROE, finance vice president, Carlsberg Group

"Whatever you learned about leadership only works in practice when you are aware of your energy and that of others. We manage time, money, and quality. But the big game-changer, personal energy, is too often forgotten. Hence, we become easily unaware about what happens inside and around ourselves. People burn out and make bad dictions when they are low on energy. It impacts leadership effectiveness, collaboration and business.

"This book provides quick and concise advice for personal growth as well as for making a positive impact. It is a must-read for anyone who wants to grow as a leader or human being and improve collaboration in a sustainable way to make the world a better place."

—ANNELISE SOMMER, CEO, Umove

"Josefine has, with her straightforward approach and extensive experience from executive coaching, a solid experience base which she elegantly conveys as a very hands-on approach to getting more energy in everyday life and dealing with stress better! I learned a lot by reading it!"

—MIKKEL VINDELØV, global head of commercial operations, Inside Sales and Dealers, Marine, Hempel A/S

"A situation that we can all get a little annoyed about is listening to people who 'don't know what they don't know.' After reading Josefine Campbell's book, I became much wiser, and now I can—with emphasis—talk about management and management problems. Even after forty years of management experience, the book provides significant input!"

—FLEMMING LINDELØV, chairman
of Prime Office A/S

"Josefine's authentic manner, combined with her curiosity and emotional commitment, permeates this book, written in a down-to-earth and easy-to-read way. Hijacking as an expression is brilliant—we can all be hijacked sometimes and from this book get inspiration to navigate our state of mind."

—ANNETTE B. HASENBERG, CEO at
MOL Chemical Tankers Europe A/S

"Don't ruin your career by getting 'hijacked.' I've seen it happen too many times to count. Talented, experienced people get fired every day for not managing their energy. The tools are simple. Not using them can undo all of your value to an organization. I'm recommending this book to all of our companies."

—CLAY DOUGLASS, Chair, Tarida Capital

CONTENTS

PREFACE

WHAT WINNING A JUJITSU CHAMPIONSHIP AND SUCCEEDING IN MODERN BUSINESS LIFE HAVE IN COMMON

In many ways, you can draw parallels between winning a jujitsu championship and being ready for changes and challenges in modern business life. First, both require you to have personal energy, to be agile. Being agile means being prepared to understand the situation clearly, whatever kind of situation strikes. You are mentally agile to react adequately under the given circumstances, which requires a high personal energy level.

    At the age of twelve, I took part in a national jujitsu championship for the first time. I won in Reaction Course, a jujitsu discipline in which players go through 12 entries. In some entries, you're attacked. In others, you meet someone who needs help. In every case, you have to adapt and be ready to defend yourself or to be there for another human being.

The championships take place at night, when it's dark outside. To win, you need to be able to keep your nervous system calm and be prepared to act on the slightest changes that your senses detect. You must be able to react quickly, empathetically, and rationally. This requires energy and adaptability. In jujitsu and other Asian martial arts, your mental state counts just as much as your physical and technical training.

I was surprised that I won since I was not physically the biggest, strongest, or most experienced—far from it. I had been practicing for only a year, but many of my competitors had years of practice behind them. It wasn't until much later that I realized I had won because I was more agile than my competitors. And I learned that being mentally agile is something anyone can do. It doesn't depend on your size, gender, ethnicity, or any other outward characteristics. This realization is at the core of everything I do today.

If you find that you constantly must deal with challenges and changes and your work life requires an extra gear, this book is for you. You want to make the best of every situation for yourself and for others. You care. Sometimes you think about work when you are at home, even before going to sleep. You're a leader—an aspiring leader, a project manager, or someone who must work with other people who have high expectations for you. It could be that your company is making big changes or just that change is a constant factor in your professional life. Whichever is the case, you want to work in a sustainable way so you can rest well at night and wake up energized and ready for what's next.

In my practice as a coach for leaders and talent in multinational companies, where change and challenge are constant factors, I have experienced the powerful effects of applying the practices I learned in jujitsu. Through the years, I've adjusted some of these principles to adapt them to modern work life. One of them is the Power Barometer.

Modern work often includes days filled with back-to-back meetings and constant change. We find ways to thrive during transition, come up with new ideas, manage our own and others' stress levels, work with new people, and handle conflict—sometimes at a distance. We deal with organizational restructuring, transitions to agile working, and mergers and acquisitions while balancing whatever goes on in our private lives. Dealing with challenges and changes takes energy, so a key in these processes has been to manage energy, not just time and money.

My adapted jujitsu practices, such as the Power Barometer, have made it possible for people with demanding jobs to thrive, perform, and grow to reach the next level.

This book is full of tangible examples from corporate work life. All examples are real, but the participants' names have been changed. Also, the stories have been approved by the people they are based on because when clients talk to me in a session or meeting, there is 100 percent confidentiality.

CHAPTER 1

MANAGE ENERGY, NOT JUST TIME, QUALITY, AND MONEY

There are moments that are crucial, that can change your life. This is the type of moment that an otherwise successful manager—let's call him Frank—experienced the day he lost it.

Frank had been nervous about meeting the new CEO for days after his company was acquired by a hedge fund. His nervousness persisted though he was confident that he was in a good position because his technical knowledge was imperative to the company. That was also why they were paying him USD 500,000 a year. He didn't like the rumors he had heard about the new CEO's strategy, so on the first teams call, he was reluctant to say too much.

But the new CEO, Joanna, was not happy that a highly paid manager wasn't contributing on the call, so she was pushing for him to share his knowledge. Frank did everything he could not to show that he had hardly slept the night before because his new baby kept waking him up. He also tried to blur the struggle happening inside him about whether his job was at risk. But when Joanna called him out for the fourth time, he lost it. There was no coming back after raising his voice at the new CEO on a call. Any trust he might have had with her was broken and could not be fixed. Frank lost his job.

Very often in business, we say, "It's not personal, it's just business." That is one of the biggest misconceptions out there. What goes on might happen in a professional setting, so it's not private. But it's definitely personal.

Business *is* personal. You, a person, are the medium for collaboration, leadership, and communication. You are the very medium that thinks, speaks, and acts. How well you do with the abilities you have depends on your personal state of mind, and your personal energy level is key in managing that state. That's why it is vital to manage energy, not just time, quality, and money.

This example shows it well: Anna is a shooting star in a global logistics corporation who benefits from the trust of her executive management. She's the go-to person for upper management when things must get done, and I can understand why. She's smart and pays attention to energy level and mindset—her own, but also those of others. She sent me a message on LinkedIn after reading about the Awareness Matrix, which you will also read about in this book.

"Thank you so much!" she wrote. "Now I can see and understand the changes in my boss's state of mind. Sometimes when he talks at town halls, he waves his arms in a certain way, the color on his neck changes, and he doesn't listen to the questions people ask him, as he normally would. I wish he could see it too, but he won't start to realize this about himself anytime soon.

"It's a shame because everyone else can see that he doesn't listen. He's the only one who doesn't see it. It discourages engagement. Now I understand why, and now I know how to collaborate with him in a better way. I also understand how to lead my team and myself in a better way, so we don't choose the wrong path due to low energy. We can work together in a sustainable way, at least until my boss disrupts it."

Later, I learned that her company had just been through a major transition, led by her boss. He must have been energetically drained at this time.

THE MISSING PICTURE

When managing any type of transition or project, it's common practice to think within the available time, money, and quality. When Anna's boss (let's call him Michael) is under pressure, it's all he can think of.

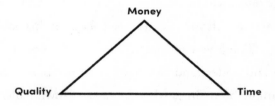

Figure 1. Money, quality, and time

The triangle of money, quality, and time—the three key elements of project management—exists in various forms. Sometimes money is called resources, but at the end of the day, money and resources are the same. A key point that this triangular way of thinking illustrates is that you have to balance the three aspects; most often you can't get all three. For example, when you order something from a supplier, you want quality at a low cost, but you also want it fast. In many cases, the supplier will not rush your order through their system unless you pay more. If you want it cheaper, you have to wait.

But a vital component is missing from this way of thinking: personal energy. That includes your own energy—and the energy of the people you work with.

Energy is a key component in our thoughts, actions, and awareness of how others perceive us. Michael is using his own energy and that of others as if it were an infinite resource, but it's not.

Your brain consumes at least 20 percent of your energy, even when you're asleep. It's the second most energy-consuming organ, second only to the liver. This is a surprising fact since the brain occupies only 2–3 percent of the human body.[1] That your personal energy level has a huge impact on how you are performing seems obvious in this perspective.

Focusing on the fourth corner of figure 2, Energy, this book will give you inspiration, tools, and tangible examples from corporate work life. You will see how leaders excel during changes and challenges by managing their personal energy and their mental states.

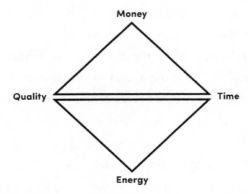

Figure 2. Manage energy, not just quality, time, and resources.

In most workplaces today, the brains of the people working there are the biggest asset of the business. The brain runs on energy, but most workplaces treat people like their personal energy is an infinite resource. Further, many people act as if their performance is the same whether they are well rested or drained. It is not. At some point, it's not just their performance and well-being that suffers, as in Michael's case. It's also their capacity to deliver quality, collaborate, communicate, and lead. Sometimes it is even their mental health. In effect, countless people are exhausted, stressed, and even burned out. Our world is in utter madness.

To solve this problem, the Canadian professor and philosopher Charles Taylor opposes the Age of Selfishness.[2] He believes we ought to remember that humans are gregarious beings who can't thrive without social contact. He wishes we would add some of our bygone community ideals to today's individualism and blend them together—as the former can't function well without the latter in modern society. If we don't do this, we risk becoming more stressed, anxious, and depressed. And we are already on the wrong track. A lot of us aren't doing very well.

For example, approximately 280 million people around the world suffer from depression. Depression is different from normal mood changes and short-lived emotional responses to challenges in everyday life. Particularly when it's recurrent and in moderate or severe intensity, depression may become a serious threat to mental health. It can cause the affected person to suffer greatly and function poorly at work, at school, and in the family.[3]

Stress, anxiety, and loss of engagement at work are also major factors in modern work life. Regardless of age, sex, ethnicity, and religion, no one is immune to the burdens of stress. Statistics show the widespread prevalence of stress. The American Institute of Stress[4] and CompareCamp[5] found the following:

· 35 percent of people globally (in 143 countries) report feeling stressed.

· 94 percent of people in the US experience stress at work.

· 73 percent of people have stress that impacts their mental health.

· 48 percent of people have trouble sleeping because of stress.

Unfortunately, for about half of all Americans, stress levels are getting worse instead of better. The Global Organization for Stress reported on this problem in 2020:

- 75 percent of Americans say they have experienced moderate to high stress levels in the past month.
- Stress is the number one health concern of high school students.
- 80 percent of people feel stress at work.
- While stress is a major problem in the US, the rest of the world is not immune to its harmful effects. Stress is a global problem as shown by the following statistics:
- 91 percent of Australians feel stressed about one or more important parts of their life.
- Nearly 450,000 workers in Britain believe their stress is making them ill.
- 86 percent of Chinese workers report experiencing stress.[6]

In my work as a coach, I often hear about discomfort, frustration, stress, and lack of efficiency in collaboration. There's a lot we can do to increase our own energy at work, but bad leadership, conflict, and toxic office politics are major drainers. Far too often, we leave the real issues unaddressed. The stress starts and our engagement falls.

Gallup reports on employee engagement show that companies with a highly engaged workforce earn 21 percent higher profit. They also get 17 percent more work done than companies with a disengaged workforce.[7]

The analysts at Gallup say the reasons for this are clear. Engaged employees are motivated to complete their tasks on time and successfully and to go the extra mile to reach their goals. They are better at meeting customers' needs, which increases sales and leads to higher revenues. Engaged employees also have positive attitudes, are absent less often, and tend to be more loyal to their employers.

At the end of the day, it is much about what takes and gives personal energy. Meaning, recognition, sleep, and many other factors give us energy. On the other hand, conflicts, endless sprints, constant changes, and a lack of recovery time take our energy away. If employees have energy, they have a sustainable resource that motivates and empowers them to be engaged, productive, and mentally agile.

The global economy loses about USD 1 trillion per year in productivity due to depression and anxiety. In the United States, the American Psychological Association (APA) surveys people's stress each year. In 2020, the title of its report was *A National Mental Health Crisis.*[8] The documented effects of stress on collaboration and behavior are also notable: "When considering the physical and emotional toll of increased stress, nearly half of adults (49 percent) report their behavior has been negatively affected. Most commonly, they report increased tension in their bodies (21 percent), 'snapping' or getting angry very quickly (20 percent), unexpected mood swings (20 percent), or screaming or yelling at a loved one (17 percent)."

In the UK, a 2018 survey of 4,619 respondents conducted by the Mental Health Foundation showed that 74 percent of the people surveyed had felt so stressed they were overwhelmed or unable to cope.[9] This was before the Covid-19 pandemic, a considerable factor that was taken into account in the American report.

It defies logic for organizations and businesses that rely on their workers' mental capacity to neglect that mainstay, especially after investing large sums of money in it. If investment funds and business owners not only optimize the businesses they buy but also boost the mental, creative, and collaborative capacity of the people who make them run, there is a good chance they will see an increase in value after a short time. Looking at it in reverse, we lose mental capacity when we wear out our people. This is very costly in many ways. Investing in the mental capacity of employees is investing in the most precious attribute many businesses have.

In my work, I coach leaders from the top tiers of

professional business life. I find that most successful leaders have some methods they use to check their personal energy levels.

In this book, you'll read their stories and get some of the tools I have passed on to them—including the Power Barometer.

Most of the leaders I work with are vice presidents, directors, and senior managers. This means that even though they have many people working under them, there are other tiers above them in the organization. They are middle managers. At this level of the hierarchy, leaders often expect difficulties to be overcome—even under unreasonable circumstances. In many cases, middle management is the most challenging place to be in the organization. It can be draining to be a middle manager. Maybe like you, they must be able to handle situations of great complexity and constant change while leading and working with people below, above, and alongside them. People may not always be fair to you or to them. So, if they want to perform over time and not just in the short run, they must have a sound energy level.

Working with other people requires you to have energy over time to be at your best in difficult situations. As no human is an island, finding long-term energy has much to do with leading yourself and others in a sustainable way. It's a personal thing.

IT'S ALL ABOUT YOUR PERSONALITY

Our personality is the medium or tool for the professional work we do. This applies in great measure to jobs within service, nursing, sales, or administration. Even a technical specialist needs to engage his personality in his work with others. Your personality is always present in your work. Nevertheless, I have met and still meet many people who believe that being professional excludes being personal.[10]

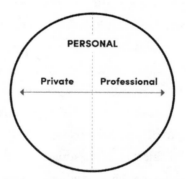

Figure 3. Private, professional, and personal

As you see in figure 3, private is often the opposite of professional. But personal isn't.

We can avoid becoming involved privately with people we have a professional relationship with. But we do still have a personality that follows us to our jobs, and the lack of one can act as a handicap in our relationships with other people—similar to a lack of helpfulness. An effort to avoid seeming personal in order to enhance our professionalism keeps most people from trusting us because many don't put faith in people they can't connect with as a person.[11]

Just as you can try to avoid getting personal at all, you can get too personal. It can be productive or pleasant in some relationships to share something private, but this is not always a solution. Connecting on a personal level doesn't necessarily imply connecting on a private level. Being personal is about being authentic. What authenticity looks like depends solely on who you really are. It's something to discover in one-on-one coaching.

Our work is a big part of our lives. Most of us spend more hours on work than on any other activity. A job is also an important part of many people's identity, and many high achievers closely relate professional achievements and results to their own experience of their value as a person. We can't take the personal aspect out of business.

As we learn about the relationship between the professional and the personal, it is especially important to understand the difference between the personal and private in the times we live in. In modern life, the boundaries between our private and professional contexts merge thanks to social media, working from home, and our strong identification with our profession. It used to be easier to separate our private and professional lives, but as soon as you identify with your position, the line is gone. So, it can be tricky if you think you have separated your private and professional lives completely. We are whole people. That's why the divider lines in figure 3 are dotted.

Being agile and in a great mental state requires a high level of personal energy, so the private and professional are both in the personal sphere. However, being agile is not a private thing if it happens in a professional environment.

THE AWARENESS MATRIX

Modern work life is complex, so it can be challenging to work with people or to lead them, for many reasons. If we're honest, we all know the most challenging situations for both leaders and talent don't occur when they must do a task related to their area of expertise. Rather, the toughest challenges involve leadership or collaboration between people. That's when the Awareness Matrix will come in handy. It will power you—with awareness—to react in the most constructive ways.

The Awareness Matrix shows how to navigate between different states of mind, not only your own, but also those of others. Anna, whom you read about earlier, wrote to me on LinkedIn (as you are welcome to do) and said that using the matrix helps her to understand when her boss is in the red zone. You can use the matrix both to understand others better and to increase your self-awareness. We'll go into detail about the matrix in the following chapters. But first, let me introduce you to it.

This matrix provides an analogy and a road map to help you on the journey toward greater awareness. It helps you see when you might not be able to lead yourself and others sustainably and how you can improve that.

Let's take a look at figure 4. The vertical axis, which we discuss in chapter 3, illustrates the personal energy level that influences your performance. The horizontal axis, which chapter 4 addresses, shows whether you are hijacked or ready.

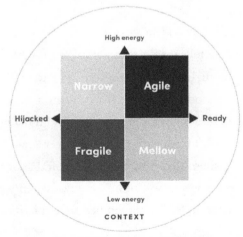

Figure 4. The Awareness Matrix

When you are hijacked, you are unaware of how you're behaving. Your brain is not capable of being self-aware. Instead, it's under the control of autopilots, as I call them. This is a problem since, in the end, it's your behavior that decides how you function when you collaborate, when changes arise, when you feel insecure, when you get angry, and in many other stressful situations. Most of the time, you're unaware of the cognitive autopilots that are controlling your behavior and hijacking your brain.

The matrix itself represents your state of mind. The circle around the matrix symbolizes the context you are in. In chapter 6, we will dive into different relevant aspects of what might be in your context. In chapter 7, we'll take all your new insight to a higher level of reflection.

INSIDE THE MATRIX

As you can tell, inside the matrix are four squares, each symbolizing a state of mind. A state of mind is a kind of mood that shows the condition your mind is in. There are many states of mind, and most people pass through a large variety of them over a day. I have narrowed them down to the four mental states that are the most important to be aware of when we talk about being agile. So, remember that this model is greatly simplified, considering how many states of mind we can in fact find ourselves in. People are far more complex and nuanced than what we can place in boxes. But to convey the meaning of ideas that sound complex and abstract, we must simplify them to make them accessible and usable.

Your state of mind colors your experiences and your everyday life. And for that reason, you can have a bad day when you get out of bed on the wrong side or in the usual cases that cause stress, such as when one accident follows another. Research in positive psychology shows that feeling happy is about 50 percent inherited from childhood and about 50 percent self-influenced.[12] This applies not only to the feeling and state of mind associated with happiness but also to many other emotions and states of mind.

The matrix has a "red" zone that we want to avoid and a "green" zone where we can live and lead in a sustainable, holistic way. Here the model is grey scale. On the back cover of the book, you can see the awareness matrix in color. The left side where you find the mental stages narrow and fragile are in the red zone, while in the right side of the matrix, you'll find the mental stages that we aspire for; mellow and agile. The first square in the green zone is the agile state of mind.

AGILE

The state of mind I call "agile" is the best square to be in. Here you are ready for whatever comes your way, and you have energy to deal with it. You are far more adaptable than when you're in one of the other states of mind. This is by far the best state to be in when you have to collaborate and lead.

When you're agile, you can choose the perspective you see people from and the way you want to react. Every issue can be seen from many viewpoints, and here you are in a state of mind where you can look at things from many angles. You can also be more creative, think logically, understand others, and accept new things. You feel a personal surplus and you can consciously decide how you will act rather than letting an autopilot in your brain control your mind and body. So, when you are agile, you can be at your best.

The word *agile* implies smoothness and flexibility in the sense that you can be ready with an appropriate and timely response. This means you can see a situation from different perspectives and act on it accordingly, such as if an important customer segment develops a new, crucial need. Sometimes appropriate equals fast, and sometimes it doesn't. It's about the right timing, just like when you are in a battle, but it's also relevant when you have complex problems to solve.

Transitioning to "working agile" with agile methods can be one of the challenges that triggers collaboration. Being mentally agile will also enable you to foster good relationships, even with people who are difficult to work with, and to turn potential conflicts into opportunities.

MELLOW

When you feel mellow, you can still be ready, but you have a low energy level. You can still be calm and relaxed, but you're not fully alert and awake. Perhaps you're a little subdued and withdrawn, or maybe you're just following the crowd—depending on your temperament. In this condition, you can recover; you can replenish your energy and renew your vitality. There's nothing wrong or bad about becoming mellow or tired as long as you replenish your energy. Otherwise, you will become fragile.

Agile and mellow are both within what I've defined as the green zone. These are where you want to be. I do all I can, though, to avoid the other two states of mind, those in the red zone. Still, I know that my brain does get hijacked from time to time, and it will put me in either the narrow state of mind or the fragile one, depending on how high my energy level is.

NARROW

In the narrow state, you can be very productive or accomplish things you've been putting off. This state of mind is a type of focus that lets you zero in on a task right to the end. But you don't have a wide view, and you're not flexible or open to new points of view. In this condition, the frontal lobe of your brain is undergoing resource failure because your brain thinks you're in a situation in which you have to struggle to survive. This reduces your ability to analyze, see things in perspective, make the best decisions, and think logically and creatively. In addition, your brain pumps the stress hormones cortisol, adrenaline, and noradrenaline into your body, severely draining your energy level.

Some people live on a well-traveled path between the narrow and fragile states. This is exhausting and can lead to severe stress or even a breakdown.

FRAGILE

Your nervous system can be exhausted from being narrow or fragile. Being fragile is worse than being narrow because your energy is low and your brain is hijacked. This means you can't be ready for anything, and you'll easily feel stressed and overwhelmed.

Even people who are gifted and are good contributors can become a heavy burden on a team if they are mostly fragile. When you're worn out, not only do you feel that you've been drained dry, but you can also drain others. In the worst case, a person can become worn down to nothing from living and working in this state of mind for too long. This is what we see in cases of serious stress-related burnout.

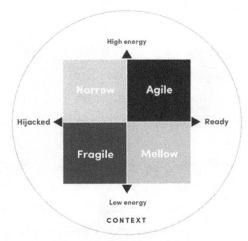

Figure 4. The Awareness Matrix

Where do you see yourself in the matrix right now?

In chapter 2, you will learn how Stephanie leads sustainably using the personal energy barometer at a worldwide audit firm. In chapter 3, we will dive into the horizontal axis, energy. In chapter 4, you will learn what differentiates a hijacked brain from an agile one and what you can do to manage your brain. In chapter 5, you'll meet Philip and his boss Susanne, who are executives at a multinational pharmaceutical company. Both Philip and Susanne are very aware of how their state of mind affects them in their quest to be agile. Though they work in large organizations that aspire to be agile, the transition is as challenging as it would be at any other large, well-established corporation.

SMALL STEPS ARE BETTER THAN NO STEPS

Even though you might not have full autonomy, you are the most influential person in your own life. You might not be the top boss who makes all the decisions, but you can still influence the people and ecosystems around you. Time and again, I notice how small adjustments in a person's behavior can propagate like rings on the surface of a lake and affect business and more. Changes in minor aspects of your behavior are a great example of how the sustainable perspective, which is about managing energy as well as time and money, considers the whole ecosystem. Any given object or person can also have a massive impact on your agile state of mind.

Let's take some inspiration from an example: A leader named Mary should be attentive to the bigger picture in her role, but she suffers from a need for excessive control of the details. It distracts her from her main focus. She misses changes and important cues from her surroundings, and it's hard on her. She wants to do well, but she keeps on missing things.

One day Mary is hospitalized after collapsing. The doctors find nothing tangible but recognize the symptoms of high stress and let her know that she was lucky this time. If she doesn't change her life-style, next time it could be a heart attack. This event forces Mary to look closely at her life and behavior. Through coaching, she now practices stepping back and letting her people do the job they are supposed to do: taking care of the details. As a result, Mary enjoys a better lifestyle, starts picking up on the cues she used to miss, and drops the ball less often. In turn, her employees start to take more responsibility. The following year becomes their best in terms of results and engagement.

For a change like this to happen, a person must be engaged and motivated. You don't have to have your life threatened like Mary for it to happen. It's enough to start taking responsibility for your own behavior and your stake in the dynamics of your ecosystem. The people around you, the context you operate in, and many other factors have a massive impact on you, and vice versa.

It doesn't matter if you are a leader or not. Everything I know tells me that we each have freedom, influence, and responsibility to be co-authors of anything we take part in—even if the context plays a significant role. In an agile mental state, we will not just be better at ensuring prosperity and development for ourselves and for other humans. We will also become better at these tasks:

- accepting change
- being innovative and creative
- understanding and working with new technology or marketing conditions
- creating synergy in a merger, acquisition, or other new collaboration
- feeling less insecure, exposed, or ill-treated
- collaborating with someone we don't like
- leading more personnel than we can keep an eye on
- accepting a leader we feel uncertain about
- doing something we haven't done before
- taking part in restructuring an organization
- changing jobs

- living with unforeseeable and unknown conditions
- reducing personnel
- solving crises
- taking on greater responsibility or losing our area of responsibility
- managing stress, either our own or that of others

BULLET SUMMARY

Now that I've introduced you to the book, let's summarize some of the key points:

- *Private* is the antithesis of *professional*, but *personal* is not.
- Amid the complexity of modern work life, it's hard to survive without knowing how to be mentally agile.
- Being agile requires you to be aware of your personal energy.
- The Awareness Matrix provides an analogy and a road map to help you on the journey toward increased awareness so you can see when you might not be able to lead yourself and others sustainably.
- Are there any other key points that you want to take with you?

CHAPTER 2

MANAGING TEAM ENERGY LEVELS AT A TOP-THREE ACCOUNTING FIRM

Too often we mentally drift off during a meeting. Sometimes we check emails or do something else even though we are in a collaborative gathering. Not only is this in poor taste, but it drains energy from the meeting because our energy is going elsewhere. That's why Stephanie's unit has an agreement: everyone has a responsibility to strengthen their way of being together. They all have to respect each other's time. For example, Stephanie and several of her employees have promised each other that they will always speak up when they feel the energy level is dropping during a meeting.

In her unit, everyone has become aware of the need to build positive energy so that a meeting can end on a high note. However, achieving this goal requires everyone to take responsibility and pay attention to the energy level in the room. The agreement gives employees the courage to say something when they feel a dip in the energy level. For example, Stephanie stops a meeting whenever she senses that her employees aren't mentally present. She is the local industry leader for government and public services in the Nordics for a global top-three accounting firm and will soon bring the same message about meeting energy to more than 350 people, most of whom are high-performing consultants.

Equity partner Stephanie is leading by starting a movement

"In my leadership team, we're using an Energy Barometer. HR has told me it's hanging on the wall in all the departments. Many people have embraced it, so it's great to experience that this makes sense," Stephanie explained.

I couldn't help asking how the barometer ended up on the wall, but she had no explanation. Although she hasn't been managing the rollout, she's started a movement, so my best guess is that some of the firm's accountants and consultants put it up themselves.

HOW EMPLOYEES USE THEIR POWER BAROMETER

Looking at figure 5 that is a power point slide from the firm, you'll find their Energy Barometer (*top*) and the checklist and examples of factors (*below*).

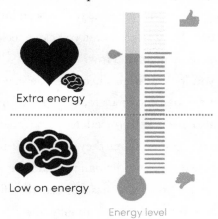

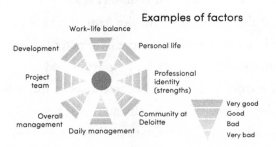

Figure 5. The accounting firm's Energy Barometer

The barometer is similar to the one you will see in the following chapter, and if you haven't already, you can try it yourself using the free audio file at the free resources on my personal website that you can find googling my name. Once you've been introduced to your own Power Barometer, you can check in with it just by following the "How?" checklist.

If you look at their checklist, you can see that they use the barometer in many types of meetings. It has also been introduced to some clients, and they use it together. After they do a check-in on the barometer, they have a dialogue about their personal energy levels. Stephanie has noticed that for many consultants, it's easier to talk about energy than emotions, which makes it easier to talk about what's really going on—whether it's in a person's professional or private life.

The factors and checklist you find in the firm's barometer offer a practical guide. It's a tangible tool that anyone can use, but it doesn't stop there. Looking at the next slide from the firm, there's a whole set of practices attached to the barometer (see figure 6) that you can use to train yourself and improve your energy level. It can become a sport, like when employees use Muse headbands to measure their brain activity while meditating. They compete to see who can go the deepest into meditation, but not the longest since in a busy work life they can often do only short sessions. The data from their meditation sessions goes into an app called Headspace so they can compare their metrics.

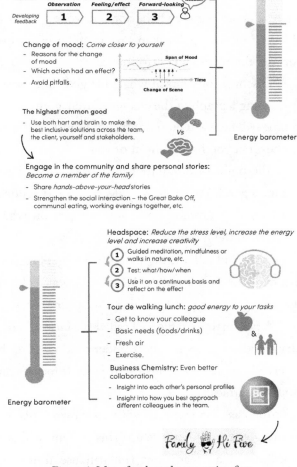

Figure 6. Map of tools at the accounting firm.

Besides the Headspace meditation tool, the firm has created a set of practices and tools attached to the barometer:

Professional feedback is a process through which a person develops professional routines based on conversations with other people who have *observed* the results of their own behavior and work practices. Give and receive feedback in a respectful way to support development and performance.

Discover for yourself what changed your mood by drawing a graph of the change. Often, going back in time will help you pinpoint the root cause. It might not be what you have in front of you.

The point of orientation is always the highest common good. We make wise decisions and actions based on the common good and not just on what serves us in the moment.

Walk and talk during a meeting to get exercise and fresh air. It not only changes how you feel but also changes your mind and increases your energy.

A personality profile tool called Business Chemistry enhances team members' understanding of each other's differences in a constructive way. It focuses on group dynamics.

You can also come up with your own tools for boosting energy in your team. This is mainly about your immediate team, but you can use it for an extended team, too, including external workers and customers.

HOW STEPHANIE HAS CREATED A FOLLOWING ORGANICALLY

Stephanie can sense when someone is feeling more resistance to her approach than others. Instead of addressing the resistance, her philosophy in these instances is to focus on those who are curious and are able to see the importance of a focus on energy. The followership becomes much stronger if the change happens organically.[13]

This organic approach is the opposite of how many leaders address challenges. Identifying the roadblocks and addressing them are normally early steps in a strategy and in leadership tactics. Stephanie, however, does it differently. She started by pulling a few people aside and showing them separately how she uses meditation in her work to create mental clarity and increase her personal energy. She then asked them to try it out at home for fourteen days.

After the trial period, the individuals talked about their experiences in a meeting. Topics included the feelings they had during meditation, the feelings they had in their bodies afterward, and whether they felt any difference afterward. The answers were clear.

Everyone who tried meditation for the two-week

period agreed that they could feel a noticeable difference. Therefore, they agreed to try meditating before
demanding meetings. The meditation takes various
forms in Stephanie's department. For example, some
have found grounding through walking, others by
meditating with closed eyes, and others by doing
another activity. The important thing is to find the
method that's right for each individual. Creating a
focus on grounding allows you to find out exactly
how your body reacts to different situations, which
gives you time and the awareness to adjust if needed.

It was only when Stephanie's leadership team
and project managers were ready to show the new
method to their employees that the process pro-
ceeded. Here they had more success than if the
change had come "from above" (specifically, from
Stephanie). Because of the tryouts and the sharing
they had done in small groups at the beginning, they
could now pass it on with their own authenticity and
experience.

Adjusting your energy level also benefits others.
This is an advantage for your relationships with your
customers and others you interact with. Overall, the
company's customer relationships are significantly
stronger today; they have, as Stephanie says, "a much
closer relationship with their customers because the
team builds the relationship with a higher energy level

and constantly focuses on building positive energy." It's an interesting side effect that was certainly not the purpose of focusing on energy management. But being able to be fully present has allowed Stephanie's department to create a stronger and healthier internal relationship as well as to increase customer satisfaction and, in turn, profit.

WHAT YOU CAN DO

When talking about personal energy and this common energy level, which employees also pay close attention to, the first thing to be aware of is yourself. If you're not, it will be more difficult, maybe impossible, to notice others.

Stephanie explained as we walked together one day: "In these times, we have a lot of digital meetings. It's very easy to drop out mentally in a meeting, so we need to be aware of how to maintain the energy level in the meeting, and know, when I lose my own energy, what can I do?" She continued, "I can easily start a meeting by suggesting we start with a meditation. In a meeting the other day, I could just feel that the people weren't present and the energy was low. Then we took seven minutes of meditation, and right after, we were back on track and had a really good meeting. But it requires you noticing. And if you do, that requires you to have great self-awareness."

Stephanie makes an important point here: when it's on you to sense whether others are present, you must be in touch with your own feelings. This requires you to be good at grounding yourself. In addition, it helps to practice noticing what mental state you're in. In her department, they do it by meditating. Through meditation and deep breathing, you become connected to yourself and your body. Sensing the way you feel to access your body's intelligence is the first part of what I call the Three-Step Approach.

THE THREE-STEP APPROACH

Not only does the Three-Step Approach illustrate how to manage energy in work life, but it also aligns with how we navigate the Awareness Matrix. The approach can be applied both individually and in a group, such as in your team or department.

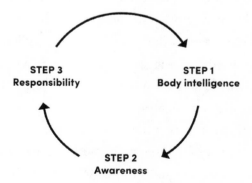

Figure 7. The Three-Step Approach, a navigation model for energy at work

As you can see in figure 7, the three steps depend on each other. The arrows between them indicate both that they are connected and that it's a circular process. It never stops. As you learn to master your energy and mind in one setting, life will challenge you, and you must start over again.

The first step is dealing with personal and common energy by turning your focus toward your body. Dare to tune in to your own body and the signals it sends so you can become better at adjusting your energy. Find out if you have enough energy for what you need to do next, or if it requires an adjustment. The next step is about paying attention, both to yourself and to others. This is how Stephanie can sense whether the people in a meeting are present or not. The final step is to take responsibility for your own energy level, and for the common energy level if you're in a meeting. Here, too, this example is fantastic. Team members have become good at speaking up if they can sense that the common energy level isn't where it needs to be. Getting to that state requires a positive approach to change, which should come from a place of curiosity and willingness.

STEP 1: BODILY INTELLIGENCE—TUNING IN TO YOURSELF AND OTHERS

The body and head are not separate from each other even though some have exactly that feeling. If you have a strong will and you feel stressed or are in pain, you may be able to shut it out, but only by ignoring what your body is telling you. Here it can almost feel as if your head and body are separate. For some people, especially those who are stressed, this has become their normal state. In the short term, it's easier to suppress uncomfortable emotions than to let them surface. Sometimes there seems to be no alternative.

When you can sense what's going on in your body, you can use those signals to gain self-awareness, which lets you reflect consciously on them. This is referred to as bodily intelligence. Sometimes you need more than just self-reflection; you need to be aware of others and to observe them. This gives you greater self-awareness, consciousness, and awareness of other people.

I recommend moderation in this practice. Don't become too focused on what others think. The trick is to store up the impressions other people unconsciously give you for use as a potential data source and then compare them with other information you receive. What others feel or want is not your guide-line, but it is relevant information.

STEP 2: AWARENESS—ARE YOU AWARE OF YOURSELF AND OTHERS?

There are different ways of increasing awareness. Sometimes a few minutes of deliberate silence can be enough. But during a hectic day, you may need more. In Stephanie's department, employees use meditation to actively ground themselves, allowing them to pay attention to when they need to increase their energy level or prepare mentally (such as for a demanding meeting).

Paying attention or having awareness is the next big part of my model. If you become aware of your-self, you can adjust your energy level faster and begin to sense someone else's energy. Being able to incor-porate awareness of others' energy levels has allowed her department to work efficiently and to be more productive. In Stephanie's department, they say, "I think I can sense that you're low on energy—is that right?" As she mentioned, it can be difficult for some to talk or to ask how their colleagues are doing since they may be afraid that the conversation would sud-denly become private and seem intrusive. But when talking about energy, it becomes much easier to have a discussion on a deeper level than one would expect.

At the firm, this open discussion has also increased employees' openness to the fact that it's okay to be honest and to show your true self. Of course, there are different ways to work around this. Some are more reserved than others. However, because they've been given the language of open discussion, an authentic and honest conversation is possible. This honesty about what gives and takes energy can lead to a personal story.

For Stephanie, this means taking the lead and sharing what takes or gives her energy. That's why she shared with her colleagues that what can really drain her energy is her relationship with her father—a relationship that could definitely be better. The fact that she puts herself at the forefront and shows honesty creates a healthy focus on individual well-being.

Stephanie said, "I also had an employee who went home right after coming to work. Through a check-in, we became aware that the situation at home required the person to go back home rather than being at work that day. We're trying to intercept private matters, too, and that's why I will be so happy the day people come to me or somebody else and voice if they have a private problem that influences their work life. If you can have the courage to be self-aware and be honest about your well-being, that's how we can create the best environment for the individual. That's what we aim for—being a team with individual needs and honoring the individual's needs to perform better as a team."

There is a lot of data to back up Stephanie's approach. Research shows that you'll have a higher success rate if you go to work and dare to discuss something personal instead of keeping everything in.[14] It's up to you to determine the level of interaction in your relationships and the way your messages are conveyed. Being able to open up to others creates cohesion. This cohesion is something that the firm had never experienced before to the same extent that it does now. Paying attention to themselves and to one another has increased employee satisfaction so significantly that employee turnover is the lowest it's ever been. It shows much greater satisfaction in work life, as well as in customer relationships. The increased attention also comes with a level of responsibility for oneself and each other.

STEP 3: RESPONSIBILITY—WE ALL HAVE IT, SO ACCEPT YOURS

For Stephanie, the responsibility that comes with this approach is clear: we have responsibility for our own energy and for the energy we give to others. The journey begins with you and the way you choose to act toward yourself and toward others. Your energy level tells you whether you're making a good or bad decision for yourself.

When we address how we feel about a decision, we can discuss whether it's the right direction for the team, the client, or the unit. It helps the team to grow together with their customers. We replace the need to be right with room for different perspectives and a desire to find common ground. We decide in favor of the highest common good rather than supporting someone's ego.

TAKE RESPONSIBILITY FOR AND POWER OVER THE VALUES THAT DRIVE YOU

Why do we get irritated or frustrated? Stephanie has realized that it happens every time she compromises her values. It's important to remember that energy is attached to every single step we take. We can see ourselves as victims, or we can reclaim our power. We have a choice to be the leaders in our own lives or to follow others and be at peace with that decision. When we get frustrated, it's because we're not leading our own lives; instead, we're following others' leadership and values, which might not fit with our own values. If we don't feel what our energy and body are telling us, we can end up with negative energy and become victims of our own lives. Our personal values matter, and we can choose whether to compromise them or not by reflecting on how we're feeling energetically (and intuitively) about impending decisions and by paying attention to our internal barometer.

Here's a good example of how Stephanie navigates according to her top value: to orient herself to the highest common good. Do you remember it from the illustration of how her team members manage personal energy? To her, following her values also implies sending good vibes to someone who is unfriendly.

Stephanie uses the method of chanting when she is in a demanding meeting. She doesn't chant aloud, but in her head. She does this to control her own energy and to be able to give back energy to others. She does it even if the person she's interacting with is defensive or in the process of lashing out. She has learned from experience that what might normally escalate into a conflict can be de-escalated with chanting—changing the focus toward finding a solution.

She explained it to me on our walk: "Then I chant silently inside my head by thinking, 'We all have the best intentions. We all have the best intentions. We all have the best intentions.' And if I can feel that I need it because I might get annoyed with someone during a meeting, then I practice chanting by thinking, 'I send you lots of love.' And those thoughts are sent to the very person who gets to me, because in such moments I can feel that I can either freak out or I can really try to send back so much loving energy. By doing so, I have experienced getting very positive feedback after a meeting. The person with whom I had a really big discussion came over afterwards and said, 'It was a really, really good meeting.' God, that felt good." Stephanie explained that this realization has given her an inner peace.

IT PAYS OFF

Managing personal energy is a technique outside the working norm, but in Stephanie's unit, it has become standard practice. What the employees in her unit experience is that they feel better, they are better at grounding themselves, and they feel a connection with their body. They are also more adept at handling pressure and acting constructively in difficult situations. Although Stephanie isn't fond of quantifying performance, she admitted that the new awareness and practices increase employees' overall performance. Their high performance is also sustainable because they are better at gaining mental clarity—even in stressful situations—as a result of taking responsibility for their overall well-being.

BULLET SUMMARY

As the case study shows, a focus on energy creates a holistic effect. For the individual, this means improving performance in a sustainable way that considers time, money, and energy. This case also highlights a new type of leadership that meets the demands of younger generations:

- Use the Power Barometer to manage personal energy at professional meetings.
- Start by checking in.
- Let people share if they like, with no pressure.
- If energy is low, talk about how you can raise the energy in the group.
- Use some of the example practices from this chapter, such as a walk and talk, time outside in the fresh air, and group meditation, or shorten the meeting and come up with your own energy boosters.

At all levels in the company, using the barometer creates better relationships among colleagues, and meetings become not only more pleasant but also more effective. It creates synergy between an employee's well-being and their satisfaction, which results in extremely low employee turnover. The last effect, which Stephanie didn't foresee, is that her team has become closer to their customers, increasing profit for everyone. As a result, they are the best bottom-line contributor in the company.

CHAPTER 3

MANAGING YOUR PERSONAL ENERGY LEVEL DURING COLLABORATIONS

This chapter deals with the vertical axis of the Awareness Matrix, energy. We'll explore the following:

- how you can manage personal energy in the workplace
- what personal energy in the modern workplace is
- what your Power Barometer looks like
- what underlying values drive you
- how you can steer toward what is right for you—even in stormy weather
- why managing energy is so powerful

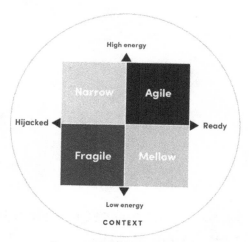

Figure 4. The Awareness Matrix

When we haven't chosen good energy sources, we feel it. Energy is one of the things we can't see, but whose effects we can observe. It's stored inside a person, and it also flows between people. We can feel it when there is chemistry. We don't need to see literal sparks flying to realize there is energy between people. It can take place as an uplifting transfer or as a negative drain on one by the other.

When there is energy, people collaborate, perform, and thrive better. When it is absent, there is a bigger chance of misunderstandings, errors, and burn out.

Energy is made of various sources ranging from glucose, oxygen, emotions, thoughts etc. We might react differently to the same sources, so there is no formula for energy that match us all. It is complex. The point here is not what it is, but why personal energy matters at work. Let me ask you a few questions:

- Have you ever come out of a meeting feeling completely drained?
- Have you ever been part of a team that gives you a feeling of joy when working together?
- Have you ever experienced feeling like not going to work, because of the atmosphere?

If your answer is yes to just one of these, you have already experienced the importance of personal energy in a team.

When managing any type of task or project, it is common practice to think within the balance of time, resources, and quality. But most people are not working like robots on an assembly line, and even if they do work on an assembly line, they're doing jobs that require mental power. Their level of personal energy affects their performance. So, in figure 8, there is something crucial missing from the picture on the left: personal energy.

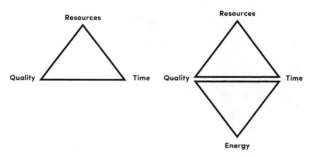

Figure 8. Manage energy, not just quality, time, and resources

As you read in chapter 1, a lot of people are exhausted, stressed, and even burned out. It's utter madness. Humans need energy to function well. Your brain consumes at least 20 percent of your energy, even when you're sleeping. It's the second most energy-consuming organ, second only to the liver. This is a surprising fact since the brain occupies only 2-3 percent of the body, according to scientists.[15] From this perspective, the fact that your personal energy level has a huge impact on your performance seems like an obvious outcome.

MANAGING YOUR PERSONAL ENERGY

Each of us has our own energy sources. Through coaching sessions, many of us have discovered precisely what gives us energy and what drains us. Energy also has many sources. It can come from physical activity, such as taking care of your body by resting, exercising, and eating well. It can come from your thoughts and feelings, like negative self-talk; mentally beating yourself up will drain you. It can come from the way you relate to other people, such as when you feel a deep connection, laugh together, or get great work done as a team. It can come from finding something meaningful and motivating—or merely from appreciating where you are in your life—and being grateful for it.

I encourage you to work with sustainable energy, which will give you a long-lasting and stable energy level. For example, sugar and coffee are not sustainable energy sources.

The following are some good options that have been brought forward by research and that, in my experience, are attainable and energy-boosting:

- seven to nine hours of sleep every night
- a short walk outdoors
- greens as a regular part of your diet
- meditation and other breaks
- physical exercise
- variation in types of tasks and working positions
- the company of people you like

· a positive attitude

· laughter and fun

· meaningful work

PERSONAL ENERGY IN THE MODERN WORKPLACE

A group of people may have a common energy level when they're together, and they may also share a common mental state. At a workplace, there is often limited freedom to choose whom you want to share company with. However, you can change your feelings about being with someone, which can affect your own energy level. Through your behavior, you can influence the common energy level because it costs a lot of energy to be negative, while laughing together increases your energy. However, this isn't always easy to practice, and some people require more energy to be with than others.

Working from home has created a lot of benefits: saving time spent on transportation, increasing flexibility, and increasing some aspects of productivity. But it has also brought challenges, such as in leading and collaborating sustainably as part of a hybrid team. These are some behaviors that create short-term productivity but tax your energy, eroding sustainable performance:

- sitting in front of a screen throughout the workday with few or no breaks
- having too many to-the-point, transactional conversations and not enough personal connection
- meeting with only a few select people without the rest of the team or organization, which changes group dynamics

In the bigger picture, these practices deprive many work relationships of energy. In some cases, employees don't feel a sense of belonging. Every human being has a need to feel that she belongs somewhere and that what she does is somehow meaningful, either at work or elsewhere. As an employer in a hybrid setting, where some are at the office while others are working remotely, I would like the people I work with to feel they belong to the team and our organization not because they have to, but because they want to. That's one of the key ways that employers in the modern workforce can retain employees and keep them engaged.

Managing energy, not just time and tasks, can be a fruitful approach. The way you work and collaborate in a group has a big impact on both individual and collective energy levels. Work that gives you energy is motivating and engaging. Conflicts, setbacks, and disrespectful communication are some of the biggest energy consumers. Here are five practical things you can replace them with as a team to raise the energy level in a meeting:

1. Get some fresh air before you start the meeting. You can either start by giving everyone 10 minutes to go outside or, if you're all in the same location, start the meeting with a walk and talk.

2. Stand up and move, such as by doing a walk and talk. This can also just mean standing up and stretching for one minute.

3. Meditate together. Just seven minutes can do the job. Most people tend to feel refreshed after closing their eyes and turning their attention inward. Do something very simple and remember that it's a break—no one has to perform meditation.

4. Have a laugh. For most people, a good laugh is even more effective than meditation. But don't use sarcasm or any other type of humor that could offend someone, especially in cross-cultural collaborations.

5. Start meetings with an energy check-in, in which everyone shares how much energy they have. This lets the team connect on a personal level. You can also share why if you want to, but it's not required. To keep it simple, you can share your energy level as a percentage or just say low, high, or medium.

Respect people's personal boundaries. When I facilitate the plus-and-minus list exercise that you will see in this chapter, we most often find that what drains people's energy is violation of their personal boundaries over time and collaboration with people who drain others by being negative or rude.

If you follow some of these practices with your team, over time, you'll develop collective awareness of what gives and takes the team's energy. I encourage you to talk about it. Ask yourself and each other:

· Why is our energy level low now?
· Is what we're talking about not important?
· Has the meeting gone too long?

Quite often, knowing what gives you energy and what consumes your energy is the first and biggest step. When you realize what moves the red marker up and down on your Power Barometer, you can make better choices for yourself.

YOUR POWER BAROMETER

It's imperative that you keep track of whether your energy is high or low. To do so, you can use your personal Power Barometer, a free, imaginary tool that you can use to measure your energy level. It takes up no space, so it's always with you, and it's made just for you.

The first step is to visualize it. If you would like to see what your Power Barometer looks like, you must close your eyes and imagine it. Perhaps it looks like a barometer, a thermometer, a speedometer, or another device. The important thing is that you can visualize it with a scale of 0 to 100, where 0 is low energy and 100 is high energy.

Then, as you're visualizing it, connect to how you are, or were, feeling in the moment you want to check on. It can be now or a moment in the past. Observe where the red cursor is.

High energy may be both tranquil and clear. It may also have an excited feel. Low energy may reveal itself as tiredness, a drained feeling, a lack of ability to cope mentally, and/or a bad mood.

Some people may find it difficult to close their eyes and visualize it on their own, so I've uploaded an audio file that you can use for free under the resources on my personal website. It contains a short exercise in which I guide you to read your Power Barometer.

If you can see it on your own or by using the audio file, what is the reading on the red cursor right now? When asking that question, it's important that you don't think too much. Just answer with your gut. It can be difficult if you're a good thinker. But the limbic system in the brain, which we are trying to access I the moment, contains much more information than your frontal lobes, which you access by thinking consciously. While the frontal lobes can process only one or two impulses per second, the limbic system can process thousands. You access the information in the limbic system through your feelings and your gut – not your mind.

So, if I ask you to close your eyes and visualize the red cursor on your Power Barometer, where is it? Don't think. Just answer.

If you haven't already done the exercise above, try to be mindful in your present work environment to determine what makes you tired, stressed, or less motivated, and what invigorates and inspires you and the people you work with. If I asked what thing or person drains your energy, and what or who replenishes your energy, would you be able to give at least three answers to each question? If so, what would the answers be?

THE PLUS-AND-MINUS LIST

Often in sessions and workshops, I ask people to take a piece of paper and draw a line down the middle. On one side of the line, they must write a minus sign, and on the other a plus. Then they make a list of everything and everyone that gives them energy under the plus sign, and everything and everyone that drains their energy under the minus sign. For inspiration, you can take a look at the list of suggestions below:

- tasks of a certain kind
- activities, like going for a five-minute walk
- relationships with certain people
- the act of living and working according to other people's values and priorities or according to your own
- the quality of your nutrition
- the quality or consistency of physical restoration, such as sleep or breaks
- the quality or consistency of physical exercise

Take a sheet of paper and draw a line in the middle. On your paper, write the lists in portrait rather than landscape orientation because you will need the space below your list in the next step of this exercise. On the left side of the dividing line, you make a plus and on the right side you make a minus.

Now you are ready to make you plus and minus list. Write only on the upper half of the paper. Write down all you can think of that gives you energy under the plus, and everything that drains you under the minus. Once you have written your lists, take a good look at them and try to see if there is a pattern or something in particular that stands out. Then draw a horizontal line below your list, so now you have a matrix.

In the two lower spaces, write how you affect the people around you when you are under the influence of the things in your plus list or the things in your minus list.

Now, we are talking leadership. Taking responsibility for your energy and how it affects the people you lead, collaborate with, report to, or live with is fundamental in leadership.

Your personal energy is your most precious resource, so use it wisely.

WORK SMARTER

"Work smarter, not harder" is more than just a catchy saying—it proves true in real life. Ample scientific evidence shows that we can't perform with optimal efficiency over a workweek of 50 hours.[16] Research shows that if we become aware of the true capacity of our brain, we can optimize our mental output.

According to the father of sleep research, Nathaniel Kleitman, you can increase your productivity by taking a 30-minute pause after every 90 minutes of concentrated work.[17] Most workers don't do this, though it would be ideal for their brain. But by organizing your day with variation in work tasks, transportation time, real breaks, meditation, and so on, you can increase your capacity by far.[18] It's a good idea to take a break in the middle of intellectually demanding work to go for a walk and get a breath of fresh air. This practice is like a planned training program with appropriate rest and activity periods designed to achieve optimal output and development in an athlete. Even short breaks can give you the time to discover how you really feel about a certain situation or task and then make the right decision. Meditating regularly gives you techniques to stay mentally agile and able to make those decisions fast.

When we look at how relationships with some people drain us, we need to take note of the situation and the combination of particular people. The same people can function differently in different groups. For example, the very same colleague who drains your energy at an auditing meeting may give you energy on a training course. If you work together in a place with a healthy culture, you can lift each other up, but in a toxic culture, you may drain each other. It's a matter of chemistry and context.

You can take any piece of paper and make your own list of positives and negatives whenever you want to. It's also a great team exercise that can kick-start insightful conversations. If attention to personal energy was more common at work, organizational restructurings, mergers, and acquisitions would retain much more value. Arlene's example illustrates it well.

ARLENE'S STORY

It's common knowledge among mergers and acquisitions (M&A) specialists, who buy businesses to merge them, that the synergy they can realistically expect rarely matches the deal's potential. As you read Arlene's story, try to discern what steals energy, and in turn synergy, from the merger.

A director named Arlene experienced the bare minimum of synergy from a business merger because political power struggles devoured all the energy and synergy effects that depend on cooperativeness. The acquisition process had taken months and had required all executives to put in extra hours and effort on top of their otherwise high performance. The acquisition felt like an eight-month long exam. It was draining. Then, after the acquisition, the real work began.

"Although a strategy and a new organization plan had been drawn up, it wasn't clear who in practice should do what and which jobs would be safeguarded," Arlene said. "The executives who should set a standard and make matters clear to us seemed exhausted or run-down. So, they did their job badly, and they were blind to what was happening lower down in the organization."

My perception was that they were tired, perhaps fragile too. The difficulty in such a situation is that there is seldom time to regenerate after a merger. Instead, executives must get going with the demanding job of creating synergy and getting the newly formed organization to function.

A selling process can also be exhausting for the sellers. There's often a lot at stake, and they move from one grueling situation to another and then must show the new owners that their investment is a good bargain. There is often an earn-out in the contract, so the final payment they receive from the sale depends on the company's performance (such as over the first two years after the sale).

Later, when I talked with Arlene's leaders, who belonged to the selling business, it strengthened my belief that the time spent selling the business had worn them out. They had become so focused and mentally hijacked that all too late they discovered their own organization had become fragile. As a result, they lost a large number of their best employees, and with them, some of the knowledge they had sold to the new owner, which they needed to get full value in their earn-out.

Learning how to optimize your personal energy is one of the first rungs of the ladder in our talent and leadership development processes. Without energy, it's tough to attain self-development, assess challenges from other points of view, or show high-level performance, as Arlene and her colleagues should have. In their case, it was normal not to prioritize personal energy. However, it's sad that a lack of energy is the reason many valuable employees involved in an acquisition become so worn out that the new business owner loses them.

In a way, it defies logic for organizations and businesses dependent on mental capacity to neglect looking after and replenishing their mainstay, especially after investing large sums of money in it. If capital investment funds and business owners not only optimize the businesses they buy but also boost the mental, creative, and collaborative capacity of the workers in those businesses, there's a good chance they will see an increase in value after a short time. Looking at it in reverse, we lose mental capacity when we wear out the personnel. This is very costly in many ways. An investment in the mental capacity of your employees is an investment in the most precious attribute many businesses have.

When I ask people to make a list of what gives them energy and what depletes it, they often put internal politics, power struggles, conflicts, and lack of clarity in the minus column. An international study undertaken by OPP under the auspices of the Chartered Institute of Personnel and Development in July 2008 revealed that the main reasons for conflict in the workplace are clashes between egocentric personalities (49 percent) and stress (34 percent).[19] The same study concluded that insight into the situation could solve many conflicts. These negative work interactions are great sources of stress, which hijacks the brain and empties you of personal energy. Furthermore, stress is contagious. A stressed colleague or, worse, a stressed manager can make the rest of the team feel stressed.

THE CONTAGIOUS DRAINER CALLED STRESS

Stress is one of the greatest energy consumers, and it's contagious. When you're around stressed people, you give in more easily to stress yourself. That drains both you and others, and it will also hijack you.

Stress is a word that's unfortunately used much too often, so it's important to define it in this context:

we mean chronic tension in the mind or body resulting in illness.

Most people need to feel that their work is meaningful in some way. When people suffer from a serious, protracted form of stress conditioned by their work, most often it's because they feel they can't manage their job. They feel overwhelmed by it or they have been compromising their values too much for too long. The WHO has predicted that stress and depression will become two of the most prevalent causes of illness in the future.[20]

In coaching sessions, when we can figure out what happened and what really pushed a stressed person over the edge, the cause rarely seems to be long work hours. The person who is ill with stress has been worn out for too long, and often we must look further back than we first imagined. It's typically a result of many hours (often years) wasted trying to achieve something that he could never achieve. Sometimes the premises were too incompatible with his own values. It became an absurd project that seemed meaningless. For example, for a person who is driven by a feeling of order and team spirit, it would demand a lot of energy to make a mess of things and affect his colleagues adversely. It's not certain that this would lead to stress, but it would take a high toll on his energy balance—and if the energy drain is too great and lasts for too long, burnout can develop.

The reverse is also true: it can be almost energy-giving to go to work when you feel it's meaningful and aligns with how you want to spend your life. Work that doesn't conflict with your values helps you avoid stress. If you want to find out what your top values are, the next section will help you recognize them.

THE VALUES THAT DRIVE YOU

Here's something that can be a big plus on your list. Sensemaking in the work we participate in and contribute to motivates most people and gives them a certain amount of energy. Living and working in a way that aligns with one's own values and contributes meaning is in itself a source of satisfaction and energy—even though you may feel tired at the end of your workweek.

You can get a sense of the worth of your work by using a numerical rating for the value and the difference your work makes. Some people intuitively know the worth of their work, while others don't. If you don't know what makes work meaningful for you, you can find out.

A LIGHTHOUSE OF VALUES

Knowing your top two or three personal values can help you stay on the right course, set good boundaries, and make the right decisions. A lighthouse of values can help you when you don't know how to act, what to decide, or what path to follow. It can give meaning and direction to your life. Not everyone knows exactly what their values are and what's most important to them. Some people know their values but forget to use them in daily life, which becomes detrimental to their well-being. If you're not aware of your top two or three personal values, consider this an invitation to discover them.

In a coaching session, we sometimes build a lighthouse of values to find the direction we should go. We might do this after an experience that has caused us to lose ourselves. Many have this feeling after suffering from stress or as leaders who work alone or can't discuss their uncertainties with others in the workplace. Every time you feel doubt, you can look toward the lighthouse. Several of the leaders I work with have become so happy about their lighthouse that they've painted it and hung it in their home even though they normally don't see themselves as painters.

Mark, a director who works alone, has hung his lighthouse on the wall in his dining room. It has become an important part of how he navigates life. Mark hasn't had as good an opportunity to live by his ideals. Consequently, the lighthouse is a great help when he feels doubt about something. When we met, he was the director of a large firm on another continent, where he was far from his colleagues. We had Skype sessions almost every other week in which we talked about challenges in the firm, about leading employees of a different nationality and culture, and about personal struggles related to living in another country.

However, not only did his lighthouse help him while he was abroad, but since he returned to Denmark and started his new job, it has guided him to keep sight of what's most important. Mark hasn't suffered from stress, but there have been times of greater pressure and a faster pace. In these situations, the lighthouse has helped him maintain his own set of values, both at work and in his private sphere.

Do you know your top three personal values? If you would like to discover them, you can try the following exercise.

YOUR LIGHTHOUSE

Give yourself 15–20 minutes for this exercise. You can do it seated or reclining, but it helps if you keep your eyes closed. You can download a free sound recording at the free resources on my personal website. The exercise is a visualization that helps you by giving a little more extreme perspective of events in your life. Try to visualize the following scenario as vividly as possible.

Imagine you find yourself a good distance into the future, and today is your last day at your job. You're in a taxi on your way to your farewell reception. You have butterflies in your stomach, so you sit still for a while with an awareness of the feeling inside you. Thoughts of your expectations for this day are whirling around in your head.

You get out of the cab and walk across the parking lot in the fresh air. As you get closer to the building, you hear the hum of a group of people. Your thoughts are on the specific people you want to see when you enter the doorway. You wonder if someone will give a speech about you. What will that person say?

After you've imagined your farewell speeches, keeping as true to life as possible, you can then analyze their intrinsic message. If the speakers say something that gives you a definite sinking feeling in your stomach, it may be important. It can inspire you to choose your values. For some people, it may take a long time to choose these values.

Below, you'll find a list of values that you can use for inspiration if you would like to continue with the exercise. In principle, most values are worthy of having, so often the hardest part is not including your most important values but eliminating the less important ones to narrow it down to the top three.

FIND YOUR TOP VALUES

What are your top three values? If you were to choose one as the most important, which one would it be? Use the list of words below for inspiration or choose values that are not related to the ideas in this list.

- Altruism
- Ambition
- Recognition
- Responsibility
- Heritage
- Authenticity
- Balance
- Contribute
- Useful
- Diversity
- Efficiency
- Simplicity
- Ethics
- Adventure
- Fairness
- Family
- Financial
- Flexibility
- Understanding
- Parenthood

- Peace
- Freedom
- Leisure
- Fellowship
- Generosity
- Joy
- Harmony
- Hierarchy
- Home
- Team spirit
- Humor
- Hope
- Initiative
- Inclusion
- Integrity
- Intuition
- Creativity
- Quality
- Love
- Leadership
- Equality
- Loyalty
- Education
- Strength
- Sympathy
- Environment
- Courage
- Nature
- Curiosity
- Mercy
- Care
- Ingenuity
- Achievement
- Optimism
- Propriety
- Passion
- Patriotism
- Dependability
- Relationship
- Respect
- Justice
- Wealth
- Cooperation
- Truth
- Self-discipline
- Self-respect
- Self-worth
- Safety
- Tranquility
- Amusement
- Beauty
- Thrift
- Spirituality
- Stability
- Pride
- Success
- Health
- Vulnerability
- Gratitude
- Teamwork

- Time
- Contentment
- Satisfaction
- Forgiveness
- Confidence
- Tradition
- Well-being
- Faith
- Patience
- Independence
- Development
- Unique

- Persistence
- Friendliness
- Friendship
- Knowledge
- Wisdom
- Vision
- Growth
- Dignity
- Humility
- Honesty
- Openness

BULLET SUMMARY

This chapter is about you, but it's not just about you. It's also about how you boost or drain energy within the team or groups you're a part of, and how you can boost your energy both on your own and as a team member. In this chapter, you read about these ideas:

· Personal energy has a serious impact on the value and outcome of your work.

· You can check your energy level using the Power Barometer.

· You can also use the Power Barometer in teams to increase awareness, productivity, engagement, and well-being.

· Stress drains your energy, and that has huge consequences for life, businesses, and societies.

· You can make a list of positive and negative energy contributors to increase your awareness and take responsibility for your own energy level.

· Your personal values offer a focus for your life, and you can live better by prioritizing them.

In the next chapter, you'll read about the horizontal axis on the Power Barometer and how it affects not only your energy level but also your performance.

CHAPTER 4

ARE YOU READY OR HIJACKED?

This chapter deals with the horizontal axis of the Awareness Matrix, ready and hijacked. We'll explore the following:

- my story from the jujitsu reaction track about learning how to be agile
- a practical example from a project meeting showing what it means to be in a hijacked state
- the neurological explanation for the hijacked state
- the SCARF model of self-analysis to help you discover what hijacks you

· an example of how a manager named
  Franz uses the matrix to navigate between
  the hijacked and ready zones (red and
  green zones)

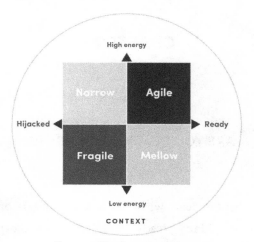

Figure 4. The Awareness Matrix

If there's one thing that can empty your energy
fast, it's getting hijacked. This is one of the reasons
you want to avoid being hijacked, but the main reason
is that it doesn't serve you in your work life at all.

Sometimes you're ready, and you perform with
optimal professionalism. When you're ready, you
are in a better position to collaborate, lead, make
the right decisions, make changes, remove sudden
obstacles, and satisfy new demands. You can be ready
to meet new developments—including ones you
haven't chosen.

At other times, you may be hijacked. You may behave and talk differently from normal. Perhaps you get a sudden feeling of being amateurish, unprofessional, difficult to work with, not your normal self, unable to adapt to change, undependable, or just off target. You may worry you're a bad leader or an unreliable colleague.

Or maybe you haven't noticed yourself becoming hijacked (in this mental condition, you might lack awareness), but your colleagues have noticed it. If you share trust and good feedback with them, perhaps you can be more aware, but most often this is something only others see but never tell you. If the realization dawns on you, it can sometimes hurt so much that you feel pain, but often you only speak a little too harshly, act too hurriedly, fail to act at all, lose control of your tongue, give confused explanations, or show other unexpected behavior that takes over for your better self. In the most extreme cases, you feel regret, sorrow, or just plain anger with yourself afterward. You might discover your behavior later and realize it came creeping up on you without your noticing. You were hijacked.

Whether we are ready or hijacked can determine whether there is a genuine connection between the conduct we want to have and the conduct we actually exhibit. When you're ready, you can more easily choose for yourself how you act and when. But when you're hijacked, your reactions are automatic and instinctive, which occurs when the alarm mechanism in the reptilian brain, the amygdala, is triggered. In other words, your brain is running on autopilot, and you lack the cognitive ability to notice it.

In demanding situations, when you are hijacked, you can react in a manner you regret after the storm has passed—and only afterward can you think clearly again. Suddenly you can see the matter from different points of view, and you regret being so aggressive, failing to react properly, or giving in, all of which are normal patterns of behavior when you are under pressure. This is common; when you're hijacked, you lose the ability to think reasonably again until you are ready. The most fascinating thing about being hijacked is that it often happens without your realizing it, and you might not even realize it afterward. It takes less stress than you can imagine to become hijacked.

Crises occur when your behavior has significant consequences in the long run. These are often cases when you are stressed, and there is a good chance you will get hijacked. They may be situations when you feel insecure, like you're on the spot, or like you've been treated badly. It can also happen in times when you do the following:

- experience changes
- are innovative or creative
- understand and work with new technology or marketing methods
- create synergy in a merger, acquisition, or other new cooperative endeavor
- cooperate with someone you don't like
- lead more employees than you can cope with
- follow a leader you don't feel comfortable with
- do work you have no experience in
- go through a change in an organization
- change jobs
- are required to do something new, but don't know what it will lead to
- live with uncertainty about the future and with lack of information
- let employees go
- handle crises
- take on wider responsibility or lose responsibility
- handle stressful matters pertaining to either yourself or others
- arrive late
- give a speech to a group

- make decisions about innovation projects or future strategies based on assumptions and extrapolated qualitative data instead of past quantitative data
- take part in a difficult conversation or discussion
- get interrupted
- try to listen to many people who are talking to you at the same time
- are ignored
- see plans get changed

All of these situations can hijack you. But if your energy level is already somewhat low or you've been stressed for a long time, you can get hijacked more easily. In some cases, all it takes is being late, hearing someone make a careless remark, seeing too many urgent emails in your inbox, or getting interrupted.

HOW TO BE READY FOR ATTACKS— PERCEIVED OR REAL

It's not outside the norm to experience unfairness or subtle threats in your workplace. Unspoken or open conflicts, misunderstandings, and bad communication are unfortunately not unusual. For many people, dealing with changes, unfair treatment, or social exclusion; losing face; and feeling uncertainty are brain hijackers.

It is not certain that your counterpart intends to launch an attack. However, depending on your weak spots, these situations can make your body and mind react just as if you're under physical attack, as I experienced at the jujitsu reaction track. Events such as feeling negatively exposed, feeling loss of control or status, losing autonomy, experiencing injustice toward yourself or others, or being insecure about how much you can trust other people can hijack your brain. I hope you can see yourself in some of these examples. If you do, it means you have a good level of self-awareness.

THE REACTION TRACK CHAMPIONSHIP

There are different disciplines in jujitsu, such as kata, fight, and reaction track. The championship I participated in was the reaction track. The concept is to go for a walk for about an hour through a solitary area, where you either are subject to an attack or have to perform first aid—all together, you must react around 10 times. There is a day track as well as a night track. On the night track, you walk through a dark wood, and an "attacker" or an "injured" person and a referee lie hidden at every station. When you pass by each spot with an attacker, the attacker jumps out of hiding and starts the attack, which you must resist. The referee allots points on a scale ranging from 1 to 6.

But as mentioned, you cannot expect only an attack. At some stations, you also have to perform first aid or there is more than one attacker. This means you can't gain points only by staying in a state of stress and alarm, in which you aggressively and uncontrollably strike at anything you see moving in the dark. Walking through a dark forest knowing you will be attacked stresses most people's nervous system and brain. When you get stressed and feel uncomfortable, insecure, or afraid, your brain gets hijacked. Then you get tunnel vision and can't sense danger coming from behind.

A sense of what's happening in the space around you is necessary on a reaction track, in modern work life, and when strategizing. From a neurological perspective, what happens on the reaction track is the same thing that can happen to you when you are at work and something hijacks your brain. Getting hijacked can be a very subtle experience. It happens to most people often and without their awareness. Actually, it's so common that it's a wonder we don't talk about it more. If we did, we could make life much easier.

Along the long, lonely paths through the woods, I practiced presence of mind without focusing. I knew that I would lose the fight if I had tunnel vision. Sometimes there were several attackers at a station, and I could cope with them only if I kept calm.

I kept my attention directed both inward and outward at the same time. I used the inwardly directed part of my attention to control my breath. When I could sense I was becoming nervous, I consciously breathed more slowly. Somehow, I realized that when I was nervous, I was not agile. Feeling the nervousness was unpleasant, and it was better to keep it away and under control by regulating my breathing. At the same time, I used my outwardly directed attention to detect what was going on around me. Sometimes someone revealed their whereabouts by not standing still. In some places, it was very dark and so quiet that I could do my best only by sensing their whereabouts in the darkness. Sensing other people in the dark is an instinct that many scary films have made use of. By consciously relying on my senses in the dark and using the self-defense techniques I had trained in previously, I felt I could keep on going.

In jujitsu and other Japanese martial arts, you always start training sessions by sitting on your knees with your hands in your lap and your eyes closed for a few minutes. In silence you direct your attention inward so you can have awareness both inside of yourself and outside of yourself during the training. Then you bow to the sensei, who is your training master. Straight after, you bow to the others in the room. After repeated practice at turning your attention inward, it becomes a natural mental gear. It's something we can all practice and become good at.

We also learned that restitution and agility play a significant role in preparing for an important performance, such as a championship. You achieve these not only by training but also by resting the last day or two before the performance and strengthening your mental capacities, using mind-training techniques based on meditation and visualization. We learned that to be agile, we should eat nutritious food and get enough sleep to be well rested before an important performance.

Overall, it was fantastic training for becoming fit in body and agile in mind. "Life is lived forwards and understood backwards," Danish philosopher Søren Kierkegaard once said.[21] This is as true as can be, but I didn't realize its truth until many years later. I just did it.

HOW YOU CAN GET HIJACKED

What is most problematic when we are hijacked is that we often don't realize what's happening, for two reasons: First, the concept of being agile vs. becoming hijacked is not a conventional one. And second, when you are hijacked, the frontal lobe of your brain becomes inactive, and your brain loses self-insight and forward planning.

You can enter a hijacked state at lightning speed when it hits you from behind. It can happen, for example, when you're in a hurry and you need to answer an email. If the message contains a potential conflict and you read it with a negative feeling, you might escalate the potential conflict by answering in a negative way. Sometimes it can be a trifling matter and, as we all sometimes do, you might proceed quickly to the next item without deep thought. However, if the matter is a serious one, you'll ponder it when your brain becomes clear again. I've gotten a bad taste in my mouth sometimes after realizing I haven't acted in an ideal way. Sadly, I didn't realize my error until afterward.

This is the pattern for how it happens, unfortunately, but the fact that there's a pattern doesn't mean you can't prevent it. You can practice keeping your mind agile and reading the first warnings that you're on the way to a hijacked state. As you will see, the solution is not to be hard on yourself—quite the contrary.

THE PROJECT MEETING

Imagine you will be participating in a project meeting. For you, it's an important event. Whether you fulfill your ambitions and have success with your work depends a great deal on this project. You're not the project manager, but you are a key stakeholder. Really, for you, this meeting is no more than a formality as you have already talked with the project manager, Marie, and the other key project members. Everything is settled. Before this meeting, you were in another meeting that went on too long, so you arrive five minutes late. You feel somewhat left out since everyone else is already sitting around the table and the project manager has started on her introduction.

"Welcome," Marie says. "Good, everyone is here. As you've noticed already, we have some new project members with us today. This is Martin and this is May from SLOF."

You feel a strange warm sensation in your stomach. However, wearing the right facial expression, you take a seat. Before you find your composure, you face another unsettling experience. Marie turns her computer on, showing a chart, and talks about the scope of the project, its aim, and the resources allocated. The project scope has changed now to include the areas of work under the two new project members. A thought comes into your head: This is not a decision we've made. I won't let them take any of my resources away from me!

I had a session with Thomas, a vice president at a large firm who had experienced a similar situation and had evidently gotten into a hijacked state. Thomas described the meeting for me. We visualized it step by step on the blackboard, and I asked him at what point he became hijacked.

He answered the question promptly. "It was when I saw the new slide. We had agreed on what should be done, so it took me completely by surprise."

I asked if he was already in a hijacked state when he entered the room. We had worked on keeping out in front with everything, and I knew Thomas would feel stressed because of his late arrival. Moreover, he had been working under stress recently. It didn't take long for him to acknowledge that this had probably been the case. I gave him a little time to digest it and we talked about other, similar situations because Thomas was unfortunately very quick to close up like a clam.

We discovered during our conversations that his clamming up often occurred because of the insecurity and uncertainty he felt toward others and his struggle with trusting them. Thomas's colleagues had provided so much feedback about his defensive behavior and reactions that there was plenty of data to support the hypothesis that this was a pattern. That is, an undesirable subversive process captured his free will and sense of control over his behavior when he got into a hijacked state. It usually happened without Thomas realizing it because it took place in such a subtle manner. So, I asked him if he knew why the new members had been brought in and if the project manager had tried to inform him. Thomas answered that, in fact, she had tried to call him before the meeting and had left a message, but he hadn't managed to listen to it.

My next question was, "How do you know that you can still trust the project manager, Marie?" Using coaching methods, we developed a hypothesis that Marie had acted in good faith and Thomas could still remedy the situation. In his opinion, this was worth investigating, at least so he could see his own views on the matter from other angles. If the hypothesis was true, his situation would not be as unfavorable as it seemed in the light he was viewing it in right then.

As an external coach, I am completely uninvolved with events in a firm. I have no agenda other than to help develop potential in people, teams, and organizations. Finding new viewpoints to solve a problem facilitates the process. We agreed that Thomas should listen to the message on his answering machine and have a quiet discussion alone with Marie. He should listen to what she had said to decide whether he could trust her or not and whether the project still meant a promotion for him—now that the project scope had changed.

From his meeting with Marie, Thomas found out that she had been loyal to him and that he had not been listening during her presentation. In fact, the project had changed in his favor. By putting his convictions to the test, he could see how his comprehension skills had dwindled when he was in a hijacked state. It also showed him how his cooperativeness and his judgment had become impaired.

In that situation, Thomas didn't know what he didn't know. The experience he gained from behaving in a practical way and having a talk with Marie proved that he had been wrong in his first impressions. For future purposes, it made him less self-assured and more humble about his convictions.

The philosopher Plato wrote that his teacher Socrates said, "The only true wisdom is to know that you know nothing."[22] Going to other people with a modest approach, as Socrates recommends, can prove very helpful. It's also helpful when you need to test your convictions in a situation during which you were in a hijacked state.

THE NEUROLOGICAL EXPLANATION

There's a neurological explanation for hijacking. You will get the details about that here, then guess at what can hijack you so you can reflect on it. The human brain has three areas:[23]

The prefrontal cortex is the newest part of the human brain. It plays a key role in sophisticated functions such as executive function and creativity.

The limbic system, also called the Labrador brain, is where many feelings originate.

The reptile brain is where the amygdala, the most dominant part of our brain, has its abode. The amygdala is the source of our survival instincts—fight, flight, or freeze

When we use our brain, we often use connections, called synapses, between different parts of the brain. Many of our thought patterns and actions are complex and require this connectivity. Most of our thoughts and actions happen spontaneously on autopilot, excluding conscious thought, and do not happen in the prefrontal cortex.[24] When we are agile, the brain can access the prefrontal cortex to perform executive functions, enabling us to do the following key tasks:

- · see things from different perspectives
- · think logically

- be creative
- have self-awareness
- feel empathy for others

When the brain is hijacked, we become locked and one-dimensional in the way we look at the world. This can happen when someone finds a chink in our armor. It can happen when we feel we are under pressure, overwhelmed, threatened, upset after unfair treatment, or something similar.

This feeling transmits warning messages to the amygdala. As the most powerful brain center, the amygdala allocates all our mental resources to fighting for survival and triggers a hijacked state. This means the brain can't allot resources to the prefrontal cortex and doesn't allow us to use our executive functions. Since one of the executive functions is self-awareness, we don't realize what we aren't seeing. Therefore, it's normal to feel we are agile and sure of ourselves while we are in a hijacked state.

The amygdala can't tell the difference between combat and an unacceptable work situation. The neurological and physiological reactions resemble each other. These are some situations that your brain may see as combat:

- insecurity about your position in the group or the reliability of others
- change, which can deeply unsettle those who have a strong need for safety or a predictable future limitations, which those with a great need for autonomy find provoking
- a feeling that your status and position are being challenged
- disagreement about what is fair, which many see as a universal concept but is often subjective and dependent on the circumstances
- unpredictability of the market or your life situation

In practice, difficult situations can show themselves in many ways. We talk about people who are difficult to collaborate with, difficult conversations, bullying, a bad work climate, etc. In the final analysis, though, most people try to do their best with what they have and manage the situations they are in as well as possible.

Most often, problems with leadership and collaboration arise and multiply when somebody is hijacked. People can be in complete disagreement, but in most cases, they can negotiate a peaceful settlement if both sides keep clear.

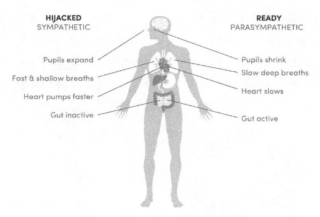

Figure 9. The nervous system's reactions

In figure 9, you can see the typical bodily reactions when you are hijacked and the sympathetic nervous system is active.

HIJACKED

The sympathetic nervous system is active and you are expending a lot of personal energy.

READY

The parasympathetic nervous system is active and you can recover and recharge.

It can feel overwhelming to be hijacked. Neurochemically speaking, the same things happen in your brain and body when you are in a hijacked state as when you feel stressed. Physical, mood-related, emotional, and behavioral signals show themselves. If you practice noticing your body's signals, you can learn to avoid a hijacked state at least some of the time. When you are hijacked, the following things take place in your body:

· The amygdala signals the pituitary gland that there is danger.
· The pituitary gland begins to produce the stress hormones adrenaline, noradrenaline, and cortisol.
· These hormones activate the sympathetic nervous system.

The pupils of the eyes change in size since an animal needs tunnel vision when it must run or fight. The heart beats faster to pump blood out to the arms and legs so you can run faster. This is one reason resources shift away from the frontal lobe and digestion. In times of stress or panic, there is a greater need for blood and oxygen in the arms and legs than for empathy and nutrient processing. These neurochemical changes in the body can also give rise to other reactions, like blushing and sweaty palms.

Mental states like focus, stress, and fear can activate the sympathetic nervous system. This system becomes active when the reptilian brain believes your survival is at stake even though nothing life-threatening is wrong—you may just be sitting and doing an important last-minute task or arriving late. You can definitely still sleep with the sympathetic nervous system active, but your sleep will not be of good quality. You need to fall into a deep enough sleep that the parasympathetic nervous system becomes active.

Your parasympathetic nervous system can function only when your sympathetic nervous system becomes inactive. It takes a little while for the body chemistry to adapt when the "danger" is over. It can take anything from a couple of minutes to several hours for the sympathetic nervous system to let go and the parasympathetic nervous system to take over.

In a conflict with tensions growing, a 15-minute pause can sometimes help the sides to resume talking with a softer tone and a better understanding of their differing viewpoints because their sympathetic nervous system has become less dominant. This requires them to truly relax during the pause and not spend the time looking at emails or social media—even though they might find it relaxing.

When you can send a message to your body from your brain, as I did in my teens when I deliberately breathed slowly while walking through the dark wood, it can help you stay agile. Breathing is the sole vital function over which you can exercise control.

When you breathe calmly, you send messages to your brain that there is no danger and it can stop producing stress hormones.

Here's a list of bodily signals you can use to recognize whether you are mentally hijacked or producing too much cortisol and adrenaline. The same neurochemical process takes place in your brain and your body, but its significance can differ. The signals may be brief, like when your palms are sweaty and your stomach hurts before a big performance, or they can be protracted, like when you have slept badly and felt irritable for several weeks. If you feel severely afflicted, you should consult your physician. The signals are the body's way of intelligently informing you when something is wrong.

PHYSICAL SIGNALS

- Headache
- Heart palpitation
- High blood pressure
- Trembling hands
- Bodily distress
- Tension and pain
- Superficial breathing
- Weight on the chest
- Insomnia or disturbed sleep
- Prickly sensation in hands and legs
- Dizziness
- Stomach pains
- Diarrhea
- Sexual apathy
- Lack of appetite
- Worsening of chronic illness

EMOTIONS

- Threatened
- Under pressure
- Vulnerable to criticism
- Out of sorts
- Guilty
- Inadequate
- Lacking confidence
- Nervous
- Lonely
- Aggressive
- Frustrated
- Irritable
- Restless
- Distraught
- Weary
- Melancholy

BEHAVIOR

- Extreme reactions
- Increased/reduced food intake
- Increased alcohol intake
- Increased tobacco dependency
- Increased medicine intake
- Reduced desire for social contact (at work and at home)
- Unstable moods
- Nervousness
- Impulsiveness
- Nervous laughter
- Indecisiveness
- Instability
- Lowered productivity
- Irritability with colleagues
- Increased sick leave
- Neglect of hygiene
- Frequent physical complaints
- Decreased sense of humor

NAVIGATE YOUR TRIGGERS

Now that you understand what happens when you get hijacked, you're likely more motivated to prevent it. The tender spots that can trigger a hijacking, such as Thomas being late for his meeting and not knowing about the change Marie had made, differ from person to person, but overall they often fall within the same categories. One of the best tools I know of to get a broad view of possible tender spots is the SCARF model.[25] David Rock, author and founder of the Neuro Leadership Institute, has summarized much of the research on this subject in a model that is easy to use.

When I give lectures and when we hold workshops, we use this thinking to show what challenges are capable of hijacking your brain. In team development processes, the development of the individual team member is fundamental. A team consists of individuals. Any personal challenges that the members bring into their team influence the team's capacity to cooperate. Therefore, early in the process, I introduce the whole team to the five triggers so they can all think about what tender spots they might have. Members don't always choose to take part in the process, so the model must respect individual limitations and stay within the members' comfort zone unless someone would like to make a hop outside of it. If a feeling of mutual trust exists within the group, requests for reciprocal feedback can help to find the tender spots. According to David Rock, the most common hijacking triggers we have as human beings are:

1. STATUS

Status can flaunt itself with titles and material goods, such as a flashy car. It can also be much more subtle, using authority and an informal but important position. If you lose face, your status comes under threat.

2. CERTAINTY

Certainty has to do with how foreseeable conditions and the future are. Everything can have an effect, from giving notice about new IT systems to moving your desk or avoiding reductions in staff.

3. AUTONOMY

When you are autonomous, you have the freedom to organize and act for yourself. An example of increased autonomy is when a person's work life shifts from being fixed, such as requiring them to work in a certain place and time, to being more flexible, such as allowing freedom to choose when and where to work.

4. RELATIONSHIPS

The amount of security we feel in the company of others is one of the primary features we use as a guide. For example, feeling embarrassed or exposed in front of co-workers can trigger the R in the SCARF model.

5. FAIRNESS

Fairness masks as a universal quality, but in truth, we judge what is fair from a subjective experience or point of view.

The five elements exist in every human brain unless there is some special brain condition that makes a person different. No one can deny, for example, that fairness means something; the question is how much it means. The five triggers can also serve as a checklist if we feel that others may have been offended or may have become hijacked. If you have taken a good personality test, it can show which of your tender spots are dominant. For instance, you might have a strong personal need for control and safety, or you might prefer freedom and autonomy.

Your state of mind can also affect how and when you become hijacked. Your convictions and mental framework can influence latent mechanisms in your thought processes and in the way you become hijacked. Trauma can have an influence as well. No two people are completely the same, and no two people handle trauma in exactly the same way. If you have had a traumatic experience, it does not necessarily mean you fall victim to a hijacked state of mind more easily.

It doesn't always take a lot to trigger a state of alarm in your brain and hijack you. As I described earlier, you will be hijacked more easily if you feel overwhelmed, burdened, tired, stressed, or somehow vulnerable.

It's seldom only one thing that hijacks you; often, it's a combination of factors. In Thomas's case, he arrived late for the meeting, was missing key information, and didn't use his mental capacity because he had been under pressure for some time. A breach of confidence can also contribute to hijacking because it makes it harder for you to keep tranquil and agile. Sometimes fewer triggers are needed, sometimes more. Some people easily enter a hijacked state, whereas others are more resistant.

FRANZ'S EXAMPLE—HOW TO NAVIGATE INTO THE GREEN ZONE

I once worked with a management team, and a leader named Franz told me at a meeting that he was feeling run-down. He believed he had suffered from stress earlier and had not taken sick leave. His colleagues considered him a champ but reserved and a little rash. Although he didn't use the word *narrow*, his behavior in many situations matched the mental category of narrowness. This came out in an open discussion during the first workshop with the management group.

Franz had his guard up and seemed reluctant to give information about the firm's finances. His colleagues wanted him to share more of his knowledge and offer them more help in their departments. Franz wasn't willing to do this. But by keeping track of when he felt he was in the red zone (the left side of the matrix with the narrow and fragile states of mind) and when he was in the green zone (the right side of the matrix with the agile and mellow states of mind), he could adjust his behavior to be more cooperative.

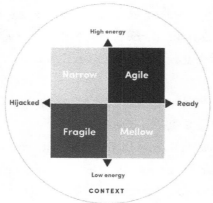

Figure 4. The Awareness Matrix.

Remember, the Awareness Matrix is divided into a red zone and a green zone. In the red zone, you are hijacked, and in the green zone, you are ready. When he was in the green zone, it was easier for Franz to cooperate with his administrative colleagues. He could listen to them, accept their viewpoints and opinions, and get them to agree with his own, and together they could find the best strategies for the whole firm. But when Franz was in the red zone, he would begin by telling them his conclusion and then spend a lot of energy arguing with them, which sometimes ended in an outright conflict. Franz himself said that personal conflicts with his colleagues took most of his energy. They consumed too much of his total energy balance.

Not only did being in the red zone deprive Franz of his energy, but it also slammed the lid down on his true capabilities and potential. When I got to know Franz and he introduced me to his way of thinking, I realized how visionary he really was and what a great high-level leader he could be. However, he had to stay in the green zone not only to realize that potential and to show it to others, but to reveal his better self as a leader, colleague, and associate. You cannot evolve when you are in the red zone. Finding a way to know when you are in the red zone and understand how you got there is the first step in your development.

To hear more about outside views of his behavior, Franz asked a couple of his colleagues in the administration for their feedback. He asked them if they would spend thirty minutes or an hour giving him feedback about his behavior. They all said they would willingly devote an hour. When they arrived at the meeting, Franz told them what he wanted feedback on. He said he had come to realize he behaved in a reserved way, wasn't sufficiently informative, and was very defensive. He wanted to change this. He asked them to answer these questions:

· Could they recognize this picture?
· How had they experienced it?
· Had they noticed any difference during the past three months as he made an effort to change his behavior?

They had seen a difference. When they gave their feedback, they succeeded in telling him about their observations in a respectful way—without saying "You are . . ." Instead, they said, "I experienced that it was not easy to speak up." Their feedback was very reassuring and helpful to Franz.

Today Franz has a mantra: he must begin and end the day in the green zone. He has adjusted his ambitions a lot and won a better relationship with his colleagues. In the end, he contributes greater value to the firm.

BULLET SUMMARY

In this chapter, you have read about what it means to be hijacked and what it means to be agile. You have seen it in these forms:

- an example from Thomas's project meeting showing a hijacking at work
- a neurological explanation of hijacking and how it affects the sympathetic and parasympathetic nervous systems
- the SCARF model and body signals you can use to find your trigger points and situations that hijack you
- how Franz uses the matrix to avoid becoming hijacked and be a better leader and colleague— and how he uses the red and green zones to simplify it

If you already have an idea of what hijacks you, you have increased your awareness.

On the path to self-improvement, you can start by observing yourself open-mindedly to see if you get signals from your body or by asking others for feedback. Perhaps their opinions of your behavior when you are unaware differ from what you imagine.

CHAPTER 5

STAYING AWARE IN A
HIGH-INNOVATION ENVIRONMENT

Philip is corporate vice president at a global pharmaceutical company. During the last six years, he and
his staff have brought about countless innovations,
which overall have led to considerable savings. They
have redefined many of their processes and methods
for building factories with regional partners around
the world. Redefining a process often involves
removing steps and requirements and making the
organization leaner. For example, they minimized
the requirements for creating reports after they
discovered that many of the quantities they needed
were already in the records. Consequently, there was
no reason to ask their markets to use resources to
report them.

As they are innovating, they are constantly launching experiments. Among these are a virtual factory and a project with delivery by drones in Rwanda, but there are also much more down-to-earth measures. For example, once an observant employee discovered that they were sourcing a basic ingredient from Norway to produce a drug in North Africa. However, the ingredient originated from India, and the Norwegians resold it at a higher price, making a large profit after only minor processing.

The employee informed Philip, who immediately gave him the opportunity to pursue the matter, travel to India, come to a workable agreement through the purchasing department, etc. The goal was to make it more difficult for Philip's leaders to say no than to say yes to an idea, so they wouldn't lose any chance at improvement. Philip has three tactics for leadership you will learn about here:

1. Be where things happen.

2. The person present makes the decisions.

3. Give space to others.

Philip also tries to stay in the green zone—to be agile so he can be ready for whatever comes next. Therefore, in this chapter you will read about how he achieves that. But first, I'll introduce you to his work.

Based on its market value, Philip's company is one of the largest producers of a certain medication in the world. In a little less than a hundred years, it has grown from a handful of researchers to a worldwide pharmaceutical firm with 47,000 employees. In 2021, the company had a turnover of USD 20 billion with markets in 180 countries. Philip is the corporate vice president of the Local Manufacturing department. This department supervises the construction of factories and the production of pharmaceutical products in conjunction with local partners. It consists of 750 employees working in nine countries but might soon recruit many more.

Philip has the courage to take chances and do what he feels is right. He follows his values and his passion for innovation, and he has no doubt or concerns about what matters to him. His driving force is that all who are in need of the medication should be able to get it—no matter how remote their residence.

Philip is also enthusiastic about stimulating progress and helping the company to adapt from a supertanker of a company to an innovative business enterprise that can act with agility—quickly and flexibly. This can be a challenge because large organizations that are structured hierarchically often react slower than small organizations with a flat structure. When I describe Philip as a proponent of agility,

I don't mean he has led his organization simply to use processes from the agility toolbox. Like me, he doesn't believe a team automatically becomes agile by learning about the technical aspects of using agile tools. Philip believes the key to agility is in learning how to learn together. Foremost, team members need to have an agile mindset, exemplified by curiosity, and agile behavior, which makes them investigative and questioning. In this way, they can continuously develop and expand the limits of their work capacity. Because of this outlook, Philip's team has optimized and developed their department.

BE WHERE THINGS HAPPEN

Philip gives his plant directors a lot of space to make their own decisions, but he also engages in what goes on. In this way, the agility in his leadership style is about stepping back and letting his middle managers manage, and at the right time, stepping in closely to put his hands on the machinery. Figuring out the right time is the art here. It helps when his middle managers proactively ask for support, but sometimes he also engages before they ask.

Philip's previous leader, Susanne, was a senior vice president. She was in this position for more than four years and describes Philip as "a perfect match for the job" because his duties in Local Manufacturing are manifold and difficult, and if you look at his CV, the leitmotif is his difficult duties under foreign skies. She told me that she sees Philip like the legendary cunning, resourceful, and fearless cowboy who's always on his way to another mission or adventure as he travels to the various factories, solving problems.

"Philip is one of the leaders who has many travel days," she said. "He is present at the factories to see what is happening, in direct dialogue with his stakeholders and colleagues—and he loves it."

The core of the business in the Local Manufacturing department is factory production. It relates to physical machinery, packaging, safety, and physical presence—processes that can't just be handled on a video call. Nevertheless, Philip is experimenting with a virtual factory and other innovative approaches designed to make traveling less necessary.

THE PERSON PRESENT MAKES THE DECISIONS

Philip has an informal manner. He talks with everybody in the organization. When he travels the world and visits factories, he's always out to see what is going on there. He believes it's vital for a leader to be where things happen. Philip was a project leader for 10 years in production for this medication, so he understands the organization's operations down to the smallest detail and intervenes readily when he feels the need to do so. This tendency can be extremely irritating to middle-ranking leaders because it doesn't follow the rules of the hierarchy. However, Philip doesn't prioritize hierarchy.

"It must be the person who is present when the action happens that makes the decisions," he has said many times. By this he means his subordinates can make decisions without his presence since not everything needs to wait for his attention. When Philip shows a special interest in specific details of the production process, he's not micromanaging; he's interested and engaged. Because he spends so much time examining the production process, he receives a lot of information. This can be confusing for middle managers trying to understand who does what. Sometimes they can feel overlooked. Therefore, Philip has made an agreement with one of his leaders that he should tell Philip when he feels overlooked. They use a set phrase: "Is it you or me?" Both of them know what this means.

GIVE SPACE TO OTHERS

Philip is an enthusiastic person with a lot of energy who has the ability to inspire others. One of his leaders gave this description: "If Philip has a good idea, he can make others so enthusiastic that they can almost fly on wings out of the meeting room." Philip believes it's important to motivate, and he's a master of it. In that sense, he knows how to turn the Power Barometer up.

One of the leadership approaches Philip uses is to give his employees space. This unleashes their full potential by empowering them—giving them the opportunity to take action and try out new things. He also motivates them by telling stories and using metaphors to create strategic aspirations. Philip uses various illustrations to depict aspiration, in pictures and in story format, when he rolls his strategy out all over the world. The local directors must apply the strategy stories to their own context, whether in Russia or Algeria. It's a stroke of genius for Philip, as human memory attaches itself more easily to stories and pictures than to long explanations of what we need to do. It's more motivating to make one's own interpretations, and this makes it easier for the local directors to be open-minded toward the implementation of the strategy. It makes them more agile.

For Philip, it's the dialogue about the metaphor that creates value and not the metaphor itself. You can interpret the metaphor in a variety of ways, and he encourages people to do so. What is right in France is not necessarily right in Iran. The confident relationship that develops from the dialogue helps to support the implementation.

PRACTICE PERSONAL, BUT NOT PRIVATE, OPENNESS

Personal and open leadership is possible only when there is a feeling of psychological safety. Openness and honesty are key factors in creating the right atmosphere. If employees don't feel safe enough, they won't dare speak up. They won't step out to make decisions or experiment, either. Philip is very open and personal as a leader, but not on a private level. Employees don't hear much about his private life other than about his Harley-Davidson motorcycle.

Still, he is personal. He's authentic and says what he means even when it's controversial or against the norm. The company has trained leaders in feedback techniques for years. In many parts of the organization, it's integrated into the culture. In some feedback techniques, the sandwich principle is central: give some positive feedback before mentioning something that can be done better, and then end with another positive message.[26]

Although the sandwich principle of feedback communication is almost a part of the alphabet in the company's jargon, Philip has abandoned the practice of giving positive, appreciative feedback first and the developmental feedback that some experience as negative in the middle. He believes it can make his message ambiguous and leave his listener confused about whether they have received praise or criticism. He once experienced this confusion himself after receiving feedback that was so imprecise, he wasn't sure how to interpret it. As a result, when he gives feedback, he jumps straight to the main message.

Philip is open and personal, but not soft or private. Part of his openness and honesty derives from the fact that he doesn't hide his mood. Sometimes he can show great irritation. Philip says he can indeed be hijacked and end up in a corner about something that irritates him. Staff members can see from the way he looks that they need to choose the right moment to talk to him rather than doing it when they don't feel sure of themselves. Conversely, employees who can't take this approach show reticence. In the first group are some employees who can help him clear up his mood. He told me about one he worked with for a long time who used to say, "Let's say good morning again." Then they started all over—with better energy and a clear brain.

HOW PHILIP NAVIGATES THE MATRIX

Philip no doubt feels tired after a week of work, but he has a generally high energy level that gets nourished when he pursues his studies (he holds a PhD) and has stimulating discourse with other people, such as his friends and former colleagues, who are good sparring partners. It's evident that Philip is physically fit, so I expected him to talk about food and exercise when I asked about the secret of his high energy level. However, intellectual stimulus and his values are what refresh his energy.

He told me he had felt more tired on Fridays when he worked in China, where the values tend to be very different from his own and where his ardent commitment could both exhaust him and force him up against a wall if things did not go the way he wanted. These must be the circumstances that hijack Philip, putting him in more a narrow condition than a fragile one. He is too conscious of his energy level to allow matters to take such a drastic turn that he ends up fragile.

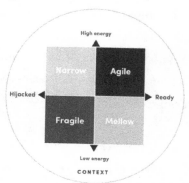

Figure 4. The Awareness Matrix.

When Philip discovers he is hijacked, he goes for a walk, for example, to see things from another perspective. There are also people around him with whom he has developed a relationship who can give him a code if he is hijacked, just like the middle manager who said, "Is it you or me?" and the leader who used to say, "Let's say good morning again."

TRUSTFUL CONTEXT

Both Philip and Susanne prefer to show so much openness that they sometimes think out loud in order to draw their subordinates into their decision-making. When they do this, it seems to invite their staff members and colleagues to offer suggestions. The valuable input augments their thoughts before they evolve from an idea to a plan. This process requires staff members and colleagues to know at what stage a discussion topic is an idea and at what stage it becomes a plan of action. It requires Philip and Susanne to be open about whether they are voicing their thoughts or relaying information about decisions.

The circumstances in Philip's context provide a solid base for him to be mentally agile. In his role, the projects in Local Manufacturing are large and difficult, and they take many years to complete. There are also many resources to handle since the company is flourishing and many parts of the organization enjoy excellent trust, security, and leadership.[27] Philip has a good relationship with his direct leader, Monica. This gives him a good platform for being brave, open, frank, direct, inquisitive, and authentic. He can count on receiving support, and if he has any need for feedback, he can count on receiving it in a direct and proper manner. This trust engenders a feeling of security.

All organizations face challenges and political conflicts, and this applies to Philip's company as well. But as far as I can assess, neither Philip nor Susanne is politically motivated. On the contrary, Philip shoulders the risk time after time to do what is in the best interests of the company—not to benefit his own career.

Susanne refers to politics as an "unhealthy rivalry" in which there are too many personal agendas to be dealt with instead of a unified approach to achieving a common result.

When I asked her what could hijack her, she answered, "Politics. It can make me very irritated, but two days later, I have forgotten it." So, when something hijacks her, she will not allow it to drain her energy for days by remaining focused on it. She confronts her observations directly, lets go of her irritation, and moves on.

Without politics and personal power struggles, it's easier to be agile. The leader's conduct greatly influences employees' ability to be agile and their behavior. As we can see from the example with Philip and Susanne, Susanne's behavior, values, and ideas inspire Philip too. He adopts them for himself and propagates them. This shows that if a leader wants openness in the organization, she must provide a good example. This means she shows self-awareness, courage to ask for feedback or use alternative methods to reveal blind spots in her behavior, and motivation to improve her cooperative skills and ability to lead and be led.

I've identified some of the behavioral qualities a leader needs that both Philip and Susanne possess:

- openness
- curiosity
- courage
- humility
- accountability
- consciousness

In her previous job, Susanne had 2,500 employees. In her job as Philip's leader, she was responsible for more than 6,000 employees representing the company's production units worldwide. Of these,

13 report directly to her. Susanne's leadership style reflects curiosity and humility. She asks her leaders many open questions, and she takes all her direct contact information along when she visits other industries to learn more. She calls these visits learning journeys. For example, she and her team have visited dissimilar industries like banks, auto factories, and cosmetics manufacturers, searching for inspiration and know-how that they can apply to their work. She is genuinely curious about what others can teach her.

"There is always something waiting to be learned so we can do better," she says. When I talked with Susanne, she used the same words several times during our conversation—words like *curiosity*, *courage*, *trust*, and *humility*. It's obvious that she's highly aware of her salient values, and it's fascinating that her values and priorities are so evident in Philip's behavior. She has achieved success with her leadership—if the word *success* can be applicable. Any leader can always do more, and as Susanne says, "The day you can no longer learn, you are on the road to becoming a detriment to your organization."

BULLET SUMMARY

Philip and Susanne, whom you have read about in this chapter, are good examples of leaders who know what it means to get hijacked, and they try to create a framework for employees to develop themselves mentally. They possess qualities to which most people aspire:

· They practice openness by thinking and talking out loud, among other methods. Their openness is an invitation to others to offer suggestions before a thought evolves from an idea to a plan.

· Their values are their driving force. They are motivated by values other than concern for their own careers, and they keep common aspirations and considerations in mind. Other people find them trustworthy.

· They are not formal and standoffish like professionals in some firms. They are personal in a truly professional manner, so co-workers can feel who they are as humans. This inspires confidence in many who work with them.

· They approach things they don't know with humility. Therefore, they are on a constant search for inspiration and new knowledge, both on their own and in groups of which they are a part. For example, they arrange learning trips.

· Today they are good at keeping their energy at a reasonable level and they know techniques to handle the situation if they get hijacked.

Unfortunately, not everyone has a good context to work in like Philip. It's not always up to you as an individual or a team member to make a change in your context. However, no matter what your work setting is like or what your leaders are like, as an individual you always have personal freedom, and you can always influence events and choose your own behavior—if you stay aware. Through your behavior, you can inspire others just as Susanne inspired Philip. In this way, you can help to shape the context and the workplace you want. Everyone in a workplace is responsible for cooperativeness and leadership.

Those with the most power bear a larger responsibility and have a larger influence, but all employees have a share of both.

It's much easier to cooperate with someone who can confront challenges with a smile—or at least see them as learning opportunities. This doesn't mean you should always resist and keep fighting in adverse circumstances, but it sometimes helps if you can shoulder your burden with a smile. We'll discuss this mentality in the last chapter of this book.

CHAPTER 6

SEEING THE TREES IN YOUR FOREST

Human beings are naturally wired to be social. As a result, mentally healthy people are affected by the people they spend time with and the situations they are in. There are exceptions; for example, sociopaths are less affected by other people than a "normal" person might be. They account for at least 5 percent of the population, and many of them have the ability to affect people impactfully. So, they matter. But that is a topic of its own that I cover in other publications. In this chapter, we will try to see your context from other perspectives and explore how it affects you. Hopefully, there are fewer sociopaths in your context. The Awareness Matrix includes a circle around the squares that symbolizes your context. That is the focus of this chapter.

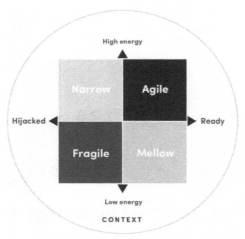

High energy

Narrow | Agile

Hijacked ◄ | ► Ready

Fragile | Mellow

Low energy

CONTEXT

Figure 4. The Awareness Matrix.

No man is an island, so you are part of some contexts. Every workplace has its own rules, norms, processes, people, and ways of doing things. That matters when identifying the right thing to do in a given situation. It is the very core of my belief that you are the expert on your own context. No matter how smart an external expert might be, you are the one experiencing your life every day. How can someone else know more about your life than you do?

What an external expert can do is help you see other perspectives on your context, using informed questions, explorative questions, facts about similar situations in other contexts, research, and the experiences of other people. But there are always small differences, and that's why you will benefit fully from reading this chapter only if you take a moment to reflect on each question as it appears in the text, just like you would answer the questions in a coaching session.

SEEING THE TREES IN YOUR FOREST

We've all heard the saying "I can't see the forest for the trees." It can be very difficult to see your own context clearly when you're embedded in it, and there is a neurological reason for that. Your brain is wired to save energy by ignoring factors that seem normal and that you are used to. If we think of how much energy the brain consumes, it's smart that we do not have to spend a lot of energy thinking about everyday things, such as opening the door to our home. The first time you have to open the door, you use your brain's energy-consuming frontal lobes. They help you think logically and consider how other locks that you have opened before have worked.

If the door does not open or close as you expect, your brain increases your focus and energy use. Once you understand exactly how your lock works and it becomes a habit to lock and unlock it, your brain rewires the brain circuit you use to open and lock the door. The brain's motor cortex is now a key center, and you can practically become unaware of your actions while opening or locking the door. That's why so many people forget where they left their keys after opening the door. They were unaware in the moment. Something similar happens at work.

The same rewiring of the brain happens to us when we interact with people and situations that we are used to. We become unaware. The brain treats the situation as if it is the same situation as last time—like it's normal not to see the forest for the trees.

So, let's look at some of the most important trees in the forest that is your work life. We'll do it with the help of coaching questions. For this to work, both the coach and the coached must take responsibility and be engaged in finding the right answers. So, your role in this chapter is not just to read but also to reflect on the questions. You might want to use pen and paper, but it depends on how you think best. Is it enough for you to read and think, or does it help to jot down some thoughts on paper? Will you want to look at your answers again later?

To see the forest, you can revisit some of the most common circumstances in your environment. Answer the following seven questions, which the rest of this chapter is structured around:

1. How do you deal with change when leading or being led?

2. Do you know how to learn in collaboration when facing new challenges?

3. Do you have to struggle to get available resources, such as in times of budgetary constraint?

4. What is the atmosphere like at work? How would you describe the people you work with?

5. How do your leaders behave, and what norms do they model?

6. What defines the culture around you? This includes norms and values that steer people's behaviors.

7. Is your trust account running a deficit or a surplus?

Let's explore each of these questions in greater detail.

HOW DO YOU DEAL WITH CHANGE WHEN LEADING OR BEING LED?

Change processes have grown from once-in-a-while occurrences to constant occurrences.[28] It's normal for a leader to have to supervise the daily work routine, implement organizational improvements, and deal with uncertainties all at once.

Today the question is not whether there are changes in the context but how you deal with them. Change always brings a measure of unforeseen things to come, which hits many people in a tender spot, the uncertainty that you read about in the SCARF model.[29] Further, it requires additional mental energy to do something other than what you are used to. Therefore, change can hijack you, and it requires energy.

Unfortunately, despite all the shared knowledge available about managing change, the truth is that the vast majority of changes don't bring about the desired results. When we discuss how to manage change, it's not enough to talk about process and content, create a vision of change, communicate, celebrate small successes, etc. You must also talk about the context. It's crucial to keep the context in mind, so crucial that researchers are questioning whether much of the existing change-management literature is reliable because the research didn't account for the context in which the changes occurred.[30] For example, if the change is a new IT system, the attitude of the employees toward it depends on whether it makes their work easier or more difficult.

In one study, a group of researchers interviewed 334 actively employed people about the changes they experienced in a year. The findings showed that the employees viewed most changes as positive or neutral, but since the negative experiences were given a higher weight (a negative experience had a weight of 3, while a positive experience had a weight of 1), the overall result was negative. However, the positivity or negativity of a change is not the sole factor in employees' assessment of it. A climate of trust or distrust, in which employees either trust each other or don't know what others will say or do behind their back, is another factor that affects the context. The study also showed that the frequency of change is a decisive factor. There is simply a limit to how many changes most people can swallow at a time.[31]

Beyond those factors, a person's individual capacity for dealing with uncertainty influences their perspective on change. Most people do not deal well with uncertainty because reacting to uncertainty with caution and worry is also part of our brain's wiring. Imagine having to survive as a human tribe 7,000 years ago. There was little upside to walking 100 miles away to find prey and edible vegetation, compared to staying in the area you knew—unless you were chased away by a more powerful and dangerous tribe. We still react as if that is our context today.

· Are many changes taking place in your
  work life?

- If so, how do you deal with these changes when leading or being led?
- How does that affect your behavior?
- How does your behavior affect the people around you?

DO YOU KNOW HOW TO LEARN IN COLLABORATION WHEN FACING NEW CHALLENGES?

When facing new challenges, it is tempting to adapt old solutions rather than come up with new ones. Our brains tend to prefer known solutions. They seem less risky. But that is where many leaders fail, because many of today's challenges are new. They require us to explore and learn together to find the right solutions. They are not what I would call technical challenges; instead, they are adaptive.

Ron Heifetz and Donald Laurie, two professors at Harvard University, have provided useful information regarding change management.[32] They define a technical challenge as one that can be solved by a known process, and an adaptive challenge as one that requires research and new knowledge.

You can differentiate between challenges by asking yourself the question: "Are the problem's definition and solution already known?" If the answer is yes, it's a technical challenge. If no, it's an adaptive challenge. Most problems are a combination of technical and adaptive.

For example, digitalizing a value chain is a challenge with many aspects that may be either technical or adaptive. It could be a technical challenge for a rental service to have sensors placed on all its products, while it would be an adaptive challenge to use artificial intelligence (AI) to optimize maintenance processes. There will certainly be experts who can explain exactly how to place the sensors and make them function. Experts who work with AI (not technical mechanics) know that work with sophisticated technology can evolve in many directions after the first iteration. It's impossible to anticipate how the process will develop and exactly where it will end. The experts may have their own ideas about it, but if they seem too sure about the process and the result, they may be overconfident, and you may want to be cautious.

The same is true for developing sustainable business practices. For instance, if you want to recycle more waste, some of the challenges and solutions may be technical, while others will be continuously adaptive. Let's say you want to trade your byproducts from industrial production instead of letting them go to waste. For some byproducts, there will be technical solutions, but for others you will have to find buyers from other factories to pay you for them. Their needs and the market for each type of byproduct might change occasionally. It can be tempting to choose a technical approach instead of an adaptive one, such as in the example of working with AI. Some organizations prefer a technical approach to a problem since this makes it possible to review the process as a whole, which seems to reduce risks. However, if you take a technical approach to an adaptive problem, it's unlikely you will get the results you want.

Typically, adaptive challenges emerge when there is a big change or insecurity in the context. Among other things, disruption and the exponential development of technology can change the market and work methods. With adaptive challenges, you need to invest time to define the challenge properly, try new solutions, perform small-scale tests, and involve the employees closest to the problem to find a solution. This can demand that some work outside of their comfort zone since both process and content are new and untested. You must go and try new things for yourself.[33]

Adaptive research doesn't lend itself only to the fields of technology and economics; a great deal of talent and management development is also adaptive. For example, becoming a better leader is an adaptive aim. In such a process, it would be prudent not to simply believe what others say. Instead, you should let yourself be inspired, take that inspiration with you in your everyday life, and test it in a secure environment so you can learn from your own experience what does and doesn't apply to you and your context. When you find things that work, prioritize them and form them into habits.

When a leader faces an adaptive challenge, Heifetz and Laurie recommend selecting the people in the organization closest to the problem to look into it and find new ways to develop a solution.[34] In that way, their recommendations are close to what has since become known as agile or adaptive leadership. The leader needs to give space, let people explore, and be open to learning together.

The function of the leader is, among other things, to give employees challenges and bring every problem to the surface—not to provide solutions or bury problems. The employees working on the problem will probably need to develop new areas of expertise as part of the project. They may also have to undergo personal development. Meeting adaptive challenges constructively will take exploration, curiosity, and development because it can take you places you didn't anticipate. It requires executive brain function and energy. So, it's key to make sure that everybody's Power Barometer is up.

- Do you have the courage to explore?
- Can you learn together?
- Do you have energy to learn and explore?
- What will it take for your people to be comfortable with an adaptive approach?

DO YOU HAVE TO STRUGGLE TO GET AVAILABLE RESOURCES, SUCH AS IN TIMES OF BUDGETARY CONSTRAINT?

When staff reductions take place, everyone gets hijacked easier. The availability of resources you feel you need to succeed greatly affects whether your brain becomes hijacked. A personnel reduction can make some employees feel they no longer have the resources they need. It can be draining and push people into the red zone of the Awareness Matrix. Further, in the minds of most employees, it creates a fear of losing one's job. It is wise and can sometimes become indispensable to tighten your belt and jettison excess weight or merely to send a strong signal to shareholders by optimizing.

However, you also need to keep an eye on how it affects the context where the work must take place. At best, necessity is the mother of invention, and employees can show their creativity when they are forced to find new ways to satisfy their needs. Still, my experience shows that is not what happens in most cases.

Typically, companies spend less money on development amid cutbacks, but the greatest need for development is in times of crises and challenges. Development can take place in the form of product development or leader training. If you have no resources to develop but you have an adaptive problem with a fluctuating market and no answers to your questions, it will be difficult to survive. As the study on dealing with change showed, employee attitudes are heavily influenced by whether the change affects their access to the resources they need to do their work.

My aim here is not to assess priorities in connection with economic measures. It is only to clarify the manner and extent to which reductions affect the context because they have a heavy impact on the atmosphere of a workplace. So, the key question here has already been posed:

- Do you have to struggle to get available resources, such as in times of budgetary constraint?
- If yes, how does it affect you?
- Can you do something to mitigate the effects?

WHAT IS THE ATMOSPHERE LIKE AT WORK?

How would you describe the people you work with?

A negative atmosphere can provoke frequent employee turnover, which is an extremely expensive affair. It also heralds unfavorable conditions for collaboration. Your and your colleagues' brains can get hijacked faster when the atmosphere is bad. A negative atmosphere makes many people uneasy. On the other hand, a good atmosphere provides a suitable background for constructive talks and collaboration to complete work activities.

Atmosphere is not so elusive a parameter that researchers have been unable to devise ways and means of measuring it. Lighting, weather conditions, interior design, and other people present can affect the atmosphere. People with considerable influence, such as leaders, have a major effect on atmosphere. A leader bears much of the responsibility for whether it feels peaceful or stressful, not only because their conduct influences the atmosphere but also because a leader can define limits that are good or bad for the atmosphere. Also, most people orient themselves toward their leader. If they lack clarity about what their leader wants or how pleased their leader is with them, they spend a lot of energy trying to make sense of every possible signal, regardless of age and seniority.

- Do you notice the atmosphere at your workplace?
- Who is responsible for it?
- Do you want to influence it?
- How can you influence it?

HOW DO YOUR LEADERS BEHAVE?

There are many definitions of leadership. A common definition from the old world is that leadership is the art of motivating a group of people to act toward a common goal.[35] But from a modern perspective, I find this definition too simple. Leadership is a social process. It requires collaboration between the leader and the follower. The modern worker is not an unintelligent follower who obeys under control. The modern worker sometimes has expertise beyond the leader and needs to be active, stay agile, and make decisions.

In practice, everyone in the organization can perform the function of a leader, and you can lead in all directions—upward, downward, and laterally. It's easier when you have the official mandate and the right to hire and fire people, but this is not the decisive factor.

Either way, in my opinion, since leadership is something that exists in a relationship between two or more people, they all share in the responsibility and influence. Those with the greatest authority have the most say, but all can and should play an active role. The traditional view of leadership is that it's managed from the top down. A leader tells an employee what he must do—but things are not so simple in practice. Although the leader has the formal authority, the leader can have employees who do not obey their instructions, perhaps because they cannot hear them, perhaps because they don't want to comply, or for other reasons.

"I really made my leader struggle until I myself became a leader," a director told me. For some people, it may be a challenge not only to learn to be a leader but also to learn to be led. A fresh graduate making their debut in the labor market seldom receives introductory training in the office routines of their new workplace. Similarly, most new leaders get promoted just because they are good at the technical work and never receive training in leadership. They often have no more than their empathy as a resource and must engage in a solitary quest for knowledge.

It's not always a matter of the employee being easy to lead. Leaders can also have employees who are constructive and well-intentioned sparring partners, who help them become better. Such a relationship must rely on trust and mutual agreement. Otherwise, the leader will refuse to listen or accede. One thing is certain: by far most employees listen closely to their leaders. Regardless of their age or position in the hierarchy, most employees work hard to find out the wishes and expectations of their leader. If a leader is not mentally agile or there is a wrench in the works, employees often need to use a lot of mental energy to figure out how to get their leader to agree with them. Therefore, the leader's behavior has a weighty effect on the organization. If a leader seems stressed or is in a bad mood, many employees will certainly be affected by it. Conversely, if a leader is pleasant, inclusive, and helpful, it sets the standard for how employees treat each other. If a leader always arrives five minutes late, it tells subordinates not to prioritize punctuality.

Bad and good leadership create context—they are contagious and contribute to culture, habits, and behavior.

When large international recruiting firms have to fill top jobs in large, multinational business firms, they judge candidates based on their ability to perform these key functions:

- think strategically
- create profitable business
- influence
- lead

But in many cases, it is difficult to accurately understand and predict how the leader will behave, which is one of the reasons so many hires are wrong.

However, recruiters don't rate one particular leader type as more valuable than another (unless they are headhunting a special type of leader for a specific task, such as a turnaround leader who is good at making large changes in a short time). There is no proof that people with empathy are more efficient leaders than those devoid of empathy. There is no all-purpose leader type that is the most effective for all contexts. Numerous studies show that no specific leader type or personality type is more efficient than other types.

Everything depends on the context.[36] Nevertheless, the ability to be agile so that followers feel secure about their standing and the company's direction will serve almost everyone because it keeps them from wasting energy on navigating the boss's mood and change agenda.

Leaders who aspire to manage energy, not just time and money, can offer employees meaning and a deeper purpose that serves the global good. Making work meaningful can boost energy and readiness in most employees. Meaning can be a deeper purpose that resonates with the individual, but it can also just be clarity about how each person's work fits into the larger picture and creates value. Most people need to understand this, but not all do.

So, what about your leadership? Do you feel you have good leadership at work? Does your answer apply only to your manager's behavior, or is it embedded in your workplace culture?

WHAT DEFINES YOUR WORKPLACE CULTURE?

A well-known quote from leadership guru Peter Drucker is "Culture eats strategy for breakfast."[37] This must mean that culture has a much more powerful influence than the conscious intentions and plans you make your organization follow when you suggest a strategy. The same is true of culture compared to behavior.

All workplaces have their own culture, just as countries, families, and other groups have cultures. Culture is abundant everywhere and silently decrees what is right and wrong in each situation. Anthropologist Donald Brown defines culture as patterns of thinking and doing that are passed on within and between generations through learning.[38] A *generation* must be understood here in its broadest sense as any group of people who share a setting. The first setting that comes to mind is the family, but culture must also be understood as a societal structure, including in the workplace and in the local community. Wherever we are part of communities, large and small, there will be different generations passing on culture, such as in the form of behavior, and learning from each other.

At the end of the day, a company culture defines what behavior is accepted or not accepted, regardless of policy. Unless your workplace has engaged intentionally with its culture over many years, the norm is a gap between its actual values and its visible values.

If you work to develop a healthy culture at your workplace, it's a given that you will discuss what kind of conduct you want from leaders, employees, and the company as a whole. If you want to be a sustainable company that takes responsibility for its surroundings and externalities beyond the mandates of legislation, the company culture has to support that. Behavioral standards also shape the level of trust and openness in an organization. If bad behavior, such as talking behind people's backs, lying, and manipulating others, is accepted as part of the game, any trust that exists will fade away.

IS YOUR TRUST ACCOUNT RUNNING A DEFICIT?

Here is a real-life example of how trust can disappear from an otherwise healthy organization. A depressed woman, Sofia, sat before me in my office one day. At first sight, she seemed friendly, clever, and professional. However, as we spoke, I could feel what was really going on. A couple of months before we met, she had resigned from her otherwise fantastic job as a CFO, and two of her other colleagues had done likewise. Their CEO had repeatedly crossed lines. Of the original seven in the leadership group, only four were left. She told me that for a long time, she and her peers had tried to get along with their CEO.

"But he doesn't listen," she said. "He meddles all the time in others' work. He violates peoples' boundaries." When I asked pointedly what had happened to make her resign, it seemed as if the mild, friendly, and professional person opposite me suddenly had a different face. Her expression sharpened, her cheeks reddened, and her eyes became a bit moist.

Good collaboration requires trust—from both sides. Employees can help build trust, but the effort needs to come from both sides. In a professional relationship, the balance of power is unequal, and the leader's voice bears more weight than the employees'. Without the leader's contribution, a good result is not possible.

Trust is one of the most essential forms of capital in our relationships. For most people, trust is also a factor that makes them dare to do something new. When trust is lacking, our normal reaction is to use energy to keep our antennas up so we can see what's safe and what's not—instead of pursuing our goals.

There are many definitions of trust. Most of them consider competence to do the job a person is supposed to do. Trust also depends on context. For example, I trust my bicycle dealer to repair my bicycle when it breaks down. However, I wouldn't trust him to look after my children even though he's a competent bicycle dealer.

When we talk about trust, we can include the concept of a trust account. Our behavior builds up an overall picture in the minds of all the people we work with about how much trust they can put in us, the same way we can look at how much money we have in a bank account. Each positive impression gives a score of +1 and each negative impression gives a score of −3.[39]

Sofia had a whopper of a deficit in her trust account with her ex-CEO. In all your relationships, there is a trust account—conscious or unconscious. The way things count in the trust account varies for different relationships and contexts. To understand the role trust plays in your context and in the determination of how agile or how hijacked you are, you must find out what adds or subtracts value in your context and relationships. Lack of trust can be one of the energy detractors. Professor Frances X. Frei and Anne Morriss at Harvard Business School.[40] Defines trust as having three apexes: logic, authenticity, and empathy.

Logic. The word *logic* means that others acknowledge you as having the right qualities and they expect you to keep your word—they can rely on it.

Authenticity. Authenticity means you have a personality that others feel represents an honest and upright individual. It is important for others to feel the person they have to rely on is showing their true self.

Empathy. If others think you are more preoccupied with yourself than with them, they will struggle to place their trust in you. You may not be more preoccupied with yourself from your own perspective, but you risk giving the wrong impression, for example, if you reply to emails while another person is giving a presentation. You'll seem to lack empathy, and this doesn't inspire others to put their confidence in you and follow you.

Frei and Morriss believe empathy may be the most difficult challenge for high-performing leaders with sharp analytical minds. These leaders are often hungry for knowledge and perhaps a little impatient since they think others can or should be able to understand complex relations as quickly as they do.

Frei and Morriss encourage leaders to take responsibility for creating trust.

If, as an experiment, you tried asking five different people who mean something to you what type of behavior fosters trust in them, do you think you would get the same reply from all of them?

· What would each of them say?
· Are you sure?
· Would you dare to ask?

I invite you to try this little experiment and see what you get out of it. At its best, it can bring more trust into your context so that both you and those around you can be more agile.

Now that you've more closely examined your trees, step back and look at the big picture that they create together—the forest, or your context. Try to see the trees that are blocking your path or are otherwise in the way. Also try to see the ones that are worth appreciating. Maybe you want to fertilize those trees.

If you read with the eyes of a leader, you can gain an opportunity to think about whether you are a part of the problem or the solution in the challenges facing you, and how you can make improvements. What trees are in your forest?

You can carry out a small test to try new behaviors in your context. Most people are motivated to take on responsibility and work toward improvement when they can see the difference their effort makes.[41] In our coaching work, we set up tests and experiments to help show our progress or to see if our basic hypotheses and assumptions have a practical result. For examples of how tests can be done, think back to Franz and Thomas. In chapter 4, Franz asked his managerial colleagues for feedback three months after he began changing his behavior to see if they noticed any change. Thomas had a talk with Marie, listened carefully to her, and tried to understand her perspective and determine whether he could still trust her. Both were willing to consider their own part in the problem without taking excess responsibility.

BULLET SUMMARY

To get an accurate picture of your own context, you must strike the right balance between focusing on your own behavior and focusing on the factors in your context. You affect your context, and your context affects you. In this chapter, I described seven factors that affect your context and influence whether people, teams, and organizations have a high or low energy level and the ability to be ready:

1. **Change.** The context has a strong effect on whether employees feel a change is for the better or for the worse. The change can result from a technical and/or adaptive challenge.

2. **Exploration.** Your context affects your ability to learn together when you face adaptive challenges that require exploration and new solutions.

3. **Cutbacks.** Resource constraints can make employees feel a sense of failure if the reductions cause them to lose necessary resources or they think they are in danger of losing their jobs.

4. **Atmosphere.** At best, the atmosphere can promote calm and productivity, and at worst, it can lead to high stress and employee turnover.

5. **Leadership.** People navigate based on leaders' behaviors. Their ability to be agile is affected by the leader's actions. In the modern workplace, leadership is to some extent carried out in all directions: upward, downward, laterally, and reciprocally.

6. **Culture.** This has a greater influence than strategy. Collective norms and values often affect employee behavior more than a communicated strategy.

7. **Trust.** You can build trust when you are aware of what kind of behavior creates it.

You were also introduced to the metaphors of seeing your context as a forest where you have to see the trees to identify the ones that are in the way and the ones you should appreciate—maybe even fertilize.

No matter what your position is, you have a role, a responsibility, and some degree of influence on your context. You can be a good role model. You can assume responsibility for tasks. You can take on your share of responsibility for your relationships and work with others to influence decisions and actions. If you do the opposite, that also influences your context, just like your context influences you.

CHAPTER 7

HOW A LEADER CAN SMILE

Mental agility is the ability to see things from different perspectives and then deliberately change your own mind and behavior, favoring what serves you and everyone else best, even if the result is unfair to you and tough.

You might instantly react to this by thinking that's something you already know how to do, but please let me challenge you. We can all do better because none of us can use that ability when we are in the red zone. Walking through a dark forest, knowing I would get attacked, I developed the ability to stay in the green zone so I could sense what was coming from different perspectives.

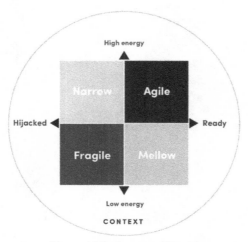

Figure 4. The Awareness Matrix.

This chapter will present a few examples showing how some of the leaders you read about earlier try to stay mentally agile. You'll get inspiration from some of the great existentialists of this century about how to tackle huge challenges in a modern context. I'll also explain how to discipline yourself and question your own conclusions about others in a collaborative and administrative context.

When you are hijacked, your brain finds itself at a loss to see different perspectives, think logically, analyze, and empathize. To be mentally agile, your brain must be in the green zone. Since this is a mental exercise requiring a good deal of energy,[42] it becomes far easier when you feel agile than when you feel tired.

Many professionals can view things mentally from several perspectives. Not many can also include emotional perspectives without distancing themselves emotionally, which you must do to be really agile. Sometimes your own feelings are too deeply involved in the matter, and sometimes you lack the necessary tools. Inability to deal with emotionally complex situations can lead to conflict, stress, lack of collaboration, loss of synergy, bad leadership, loss of benefit from reorganizing, and poor results.[43] Many of the leaders you have read about in this book already know the technique and practice it regularly. You will read about it now. But first let's step back in time, into the Greek mythology that in many ways has shaped how we think in the Western hemisphere.

King Sisyphus was the king of Corinth, an enterprising leader who increased shipping and trade, but he was also greedy and deceitful. He managed to anger the gods on several occasions, such as by murdering travelers and guests at his palace. That was a sin. It violated the principle of hospitality, of which the god Zeus was the patron. Zeus became annoyed, but this was not the only misdeed Sisyphus perpetrated. In *The Iliad*, one of Europe's first historians,[44] Homer, tells us that Zeus once kidnapped the nymph Aigina.

Sisyphus saw it happen, and when the river god Asopos, her father, couldn't find her, Sisyphus made a bargain with him. Sisyphus informed him that Zeus was the kidnapper, and in return for this information, Asopos made a river gush out near Sisyphus's palace in Corinth. The water from the river made it possible to grow crops in the soil and this engendered prosperity.

Zeus became so angry in the face of Sisyphus's disloyalty that he ordered Sisyphus placed in chains in the underworld. Here Sisyphus managed to entice Death to demonstrate how the chains linked together, and in doing so, Death bound himself with the chains while Sisyphus escaped and returned to the world of the living. Because Death was in chains, unable to ply his trade, people stopped dying in the world above. This brought things to a standstill, and the god of war, Ares, became so angry that he sprang into action. It spoiled the concept of war when opponents could not die. Consequently, Ares imprisoned Sisyphus and turned him over to Death.

A second time, Sisyphus contrived to escape from Death. This time he persuaded Persephone, the goddess of the underworld, to let him return to the world above and talk to his wife because she had left his corpse lying on public ground instead of giving it a fitting burial. What Persephone didn't know was that Sisyphus's wife had acted in accordance with his instructions and Sisyphus had no intention of returning to the underworld. In this way, Sisyphus escaped again.

However, the gods recaptured him, and as punishment for all his treachery, Zeus sentenced him to eternal labor. Sisyphus was compelled to roll a large boulder up to the top of a mountain. Every time the boulder reached the top, it rolled back down, and he had to return to the bottom and roll it up again. This cycle would continue forever. From this story, we've gained the expression *a Sisyphean task*: work that seems absurd but continues without end. Sounds dreary, doesn't it?

We also compare ourselves to a hamster on a wheel, always running but never going anywhere. At times when work and hardship seem endless, it's difficult to find meaning in them. In 1942, in the middle of the Second World War, when life must have been difficult for many people, the French existentialist philosopher Albert Camus published a book that showed an alternative path. He suggested we try to visualize Sisyphus's face the moment he went down the mountain after the boulder, knowing he had to push it up yet again and it would never end.

He asked us to imagine Sisyphus's face with a smile. Imagine he has chosen to carry his burden willingly and find the beauty in his surroundings.

We always have freedom to choose how we accept the troubles we face and how we feel about the things happening to us. Camus describes how Sisyphus can find freedom by choosing how he feels about the task he is doomed to perform. Camus writes, "I leave Sisyphus at the foot of the mountain. We always re-find our burden. However, Sisyphus bears testimony to a higher belief that refuses allegiance to the gods, and he lifts the boulder. And he discovers that all things are good. The godless universe seems neither barren nor useless to him. Every grain of granite in the boulder, every shiny lump of mineral in the dark matrix of the mountain constitutes a world of its own. The struggle to reach the mountain peak is enough to fill up a person's heart. We must think of Sisyphus as a happy man."[45]

We must assume Camus's Sisyphus is fragile if he performs his toil with a feeling of gloom. Instead, he uses his last vestiges of freedom to choose for himself how he will serve his punishment. He chooses the mood he is in when he carries out his task. If he chooses to do it with joy, we can imagine Sisyphus as a happy man, just as Camus suggests—a man who is agile instead of fragile.

IMAGINING A LEADER WITH A SMILE

If our thoughts are fresher in the morning than at night, mornings are a better time for being agile than nights. When being mentally agile, we can view matters from the perspectives of different people and alternate playing the roles of the protagonists and of those standing on the sideline on the same issue—or we can view the problems from the outside or sense an attack from behind. We can take a close-up look and sense what is really going on around us or climb to a helicopter perspective when we need to. We can do this exactly as I described in chapter 5: Philip is good at moving in close, then backing off to leave room for his leaders to adapt their own strategies to the context. Let's revisit a couple of other examples.

Susanne imagines she's sitting at a table with all the people involved. Quite automatically, she shifts her mental perspective from chair to chair, not only to familiarize herself with their opinions but also to understand their feelings on the matter. It gives her a better foundation for making decisions and more insight into how much she can realistically expect from the parties concerned.

Stephanie pays attention to her energy level and thoughts about other people. She takes a walk or meditates to stay agile. If she's in a meeting where she can't just get up and take a walk or meditate, she has another method. If she starts to get annoyed with someone, she chants silently to direct herself to see them in a more positive perspective, to make sure they don't get to her, and to help the meeting to go well.

When Philip feels hijacked, he finds it helpful "to go for a walk and see things from the outside," he says. "Sometimes it's a walk around the factory that's needed. That can relieve some of the tension. Then I think perhaps it's not as bad as I thought. Perhaps it doesn't seem so bad—nevertheless." Although he's learned to mentally separate himself from any challenges he faces, Philip is impassioned and very absorbed in his work. The technique doesn't involve creating so much distance that we lose our engagement and motivation. It's a matter of looking at things from the outside.

Once Philip had a leader, Tom, who taught him and his colleagues how to be more agile when dealing with problematic issues and relieve tensions. Sometimes when they felt great pressure, he relieved the tension by saying, "Oh, in two years we'll be sitting with our feet on the desk and laughing at it."

Perspective and distance are two of the major challenges in leadership, just like knowing when to use micro-management or macro-management. Getting a handle on them is not easy if you unconsciously have a large part of your identity and your feelings wrapped up in your work and you don't master this technique. Being agile doesn't mean keeping everything at arm's length and being cold. In fact, it's just the opposite.

Imagine what it demands of a person mentally to be both actor and director in the same film. He needs to see himself from the outside and from different perspectives in order to perform as a director.

The leaders you have read about here are all in high positions in hierarchies, and some of them have hundreds or thousands of employees under them. They have, in one way or another, learned how to be mentally agile, not only intellectually but also emotionally. Otherwise, they would neither be able to understand others or endure a high level of engagement. Of course, they don't always manage to use the technique. Sometimes they get hijacked. So do I. We all do.

When a leader gets promoted, expectations grow about how much responsibility she can shoulder, how much complexity she can manage, and how many tough pills she'll have to swallow. In a high position, you can end up in the middle of conflicts in which you have had no part. You can be a target of criticism from employees, newspapers, and trade unions, and this criticism may seem undeserved, but dealing with it is part of your job.

A director I coached named Maria worked at a factory in Spain, where trade unions are very powerful. The factory's optimal operation depended largely on collaboration with the trade union, which often resulted in conflicts. One day when she appeared on the screen for our virtual meeting, I could see her facial expression was different. She was clearly tense. Prominent trade union leaders had denounced her publicly using personal, inappropriate accusations that were completely false. She was angry and insulted but didn't know what to do. The conflict had begun long before she had started at the factory, but now she was the target of all the attacks they could launch. The trade union had previously been successful at orchestrating the downfall of a factory manager by shaming him publicly.

In this example, an individual practicing her profession was personally attacked. Her personal traits and actions are tools and vehicles for her work, so it's easy to understand why she felt the attacks were personal, especially since the injustice she felt also affected her in the private sphere. You might face a similar challenge in your job. We can quickly agree that the factory manager was treated unjustly.

It would be nice if someone could take charge of the matter and correct the wrongs. But there are only two things we can be sure of: we will encounter challenges that are unfair, and one day we will die. We exert more influence on the way we experience life and what we get out of it if we choose to be co-authors of our own perspective. This doesn't mean ignoring other perspectives—quite the contrary. But if we give our own perspective only the same weight as others and we see several different perspectives, then it becomes easier to avoid feeling personal affront and getting hijacked.

This is also why only those who can meet challenges in an agile way continue to get promoted as leaders. Leadership can sometimes seem like a long string of problems that demand solutions. In many ways, the picture of Sisyphus accurately represents how it sometimes feels to be a leader.

Part of a leader's function is to solve problems: the problems of employees, of the firm, of the higher-ups, etc. It's particularly tough when you're a middle manager squeezed between layers of the hierarchy. In the role of leader, you have to face many trials and respond with a professional smile. Meaning is the main source of energy and motivation for most people, by far. So, let's follow Camus's suggestion and visualize Sisyphus on his way down the mountainside with a smile, or visualize someone else in a situation that seems absurd with a smile. This helps us make a U-turn and makes it possible to be agile when we have to address absurd situations such as the climate crisis, in which humanity is on our way to eradicating ourselves, or difficult challenges such as how to lead sustainably.

HOW TO DEAL WITH THE ABSURDITY

If you choose an example from your own life of a situation you think is absurd, can you reap some benefit by trying to examine it from different perspectives?

- Which impressions would you keep?
- How does it affect your Power Barometer?
- Does it make you more agile?

We can always choose the perspective we use to view the events in our lives and the importance and energy we give them. This doesn't mean we should leave anything out or tinge it a shade of pink. However, there is a perspective for everything, and your ability to find a meaningful perspective decides whether you can stay agile in your relationships.

MAN'S LAST FREEDOM: GIVING MEANING TO MADNESS

Viktor Frankl, one of the greatest psychologists of our time, describes in his book his four nightmarish years as a Jew in a Nazi concentration camp. He discovered there that the ones who survived were the ones who could find meaning amid the madness—the ones who were agile.[46] He called this ability "man's last freedom."[47]

Frankl later became the founder of Logos Therapy, a form of therapy based on finding meaning in things. He used his four years in the camp to study what enables people to survive under the most terrible conditions imaginable and published this study after regaining his freedom. The results showed that those who managed best were the ones who found meaning in their lives. He felt a strong motivation to survive and publish his study, to share his discoveries with the world. He also found that there is meaning in every instant of time and that "everything can be taken away from a person with the exception of a single thing: man's last freedom is to choose his own attitude in any given set of conditions and to choose his own methods."[48]

Among the many interpretations of *meaning* is the view that it's an idealistic quality, such as contributing toward a better world, but it can also have low practicality. One example is that IT functions improve customer service and make everything easier, or that as an employee I involve myself in a task to help my colleagues (if helping others is part of my set of values).

Agility is an approach that, despite its efficiency, meets with a fair amount of criticism because it relegates a good portion of responsibility, influence, and freedom to the hands of the individual. For instance, after I lectured about perspectivation to a group within a police force, some audience members felt I had given them a formula for freedom, while others didn't believe it could have any effect on their past experiences.

In a way, agility gives the individual a lot of responsibility and influence, like what Spencer Johnson describes in *Who Moved My Cheese?*[249] Transferring responsibility onto the shoulders of employees to accomplish necessary changes (like a round of layoffs or new agile processes) aligns with a perspective that has earned much criticism, and considerable scientific evidence shows it does not give good results. However, this doesn't relieve the individual of his share of the responsibility for changes, agile improvements, conflict, or other situations involving several parties. We must remember that agility must not stand alone in the context of a workplace where there is a lopsided balance of power. The leaders must be the vanguard, and the organizational measures, administrative efforts, and individual efforts must be coordinated.[50]

AVOIDING HASTY CONCLUSIONS

Complexity and multiple perspectives demand energy from your brain. That's why we often choose simple answers instead of including all the externalities we can think of in a given situation.

It's inherent in the automatic programs in your brain that you deduce logical conclusions. A logical conclusion is an analysis of observations registered more quickly than you are consciously aware of. This means you believe your thoughts to be true. When you need to be agile, it's practical to "rewind the film" and find where you arrived at a logical conclusion that may not be well grounded or can be interpreted differently. Time and again, we arrive at conclusions faster than we realize.

The model below demonstrates how we normally do this based on our observations and premises.[51] The logical results function just like an automatic program. We are not conscious of doing several intermediate calculations that may be incorrect. In our consciousness, we move from observation to analysis to conclusion in a split second, without realizing it. Here's an example of a logical syllogism:

Jonas is blond
+ Swedes are often blonds
= Jonas is a Swede

The problem with this is we often make mistakes in the intermediate calculations. We do not know for a fact that Jonas is a Swede, and it's rather hasty to judge him as such simply because he is blond. This example may appear oversimplified, but it illustrates precisely how we develop a bias—a mass of prejudiced perspectives we've created in the past using experiences from the past. This means we often don't judge what we are confronted with fairly. Often, we don't keep an open mind toward other perspectives, such as that Jonas could be Russian, British, or from somewhere else in the world despite his seemingly Scandinavian blond hair. This also means that in conversations, many of us do not listen attentively and examine what the other person really means and contributes before drawing our conclusions. We can be in a narrow state or even a fragile state.

In many work-related conflicts, people make assumptions about the thoughts and feelings of their fellow workers. In these cases, they have simply drawn logical conclusions too quickly without allowing for any complexity. If they engage in open-hearted conversations and lighten the mood, they often find that the picture they imagined differs from reality. Perhaps there was no reason to get hijacked at all. However, an agile mindset is a prerequisite for having the mental surplus to see new perspectives on an old matter—and especially to see the people you know with new eyes.

Try to think of your thoughts as having different levels of interpretation on a ladder: raw data is at the bottom, and the farther you ascend, the higher the number of interpretations and hasty conclusions. Think of a specific situation.

I'll give you an example. At a seminar I once held, one of the participants sat in the back without saying a word. He was sitting and looking out at the room with no expression, and I thought he might be bored. This was my logical deduction because people often show interest and keep their gaze toward the front when I conduct a seminar. I became increasingly curious about how I could attract his interest. What could I do better? During a pause, I gained an opportunity to talk to him. I asked for his opinion of the seminar, and he replied that it was so relevant to his situation, he constantly reflected on what I was teaching in relation to situations at his workplace.

As you can tell, I had been wrong in my assumption. He was neither bored nor uninterested, but overstimulated.

ADDRESSING YOUR AUTOPILOTS

Personal and professional development is like a voyage of discovery. Automatic programs dictate the bulk of what we do and say. When we become conscious of these automatic programs, or autopilots, and start addressing them, we can move our minds from unconscious to conscious and take longer strides.

Autopilots are like programs that run automatically in your brain. They function so effortlessly that you're not aware of them. Imagine your brain is a computer, and you're born containing a hard drive. Throughout your life, you keep learning about the world and saving updated programs. At the beginning, you have an inquisitive nature and like to play until you learn the difference between right and wrong. This tendency shapes your first set of programs, and they function as your operating system, brimming with a host of mental autopilots. However, the updates don't end in childhood. All your experiences, especially your first important job, influence how you will meet your challenges and how you will behave as an employee, colleague, and leader.

In the context in which you saved these programs, they work.

The context may change or there may be too much uncertainty about the present context, as no one knows for sure where the world is heading. In these cases, if you follow your autopilot, the question becomes "Is this the right program and the right approach?" Your program was the right one when it was installed, but is it right now? What is most difficult is not assimilating new abilities and new ways of looking at things but unlearning what used to be right. The first step toward a new behavior is to become aware of your autopilots.

A director I was coaching, Hans, wanted to expand his influence and have a greater presence in the eyes of his employees. Hans was the national director of a large, international company. In addition, he was the project leader for several global projects, so he had to be shrewd to accomplish all of his goals. He learned that he needed to be smart visible. Being smart visible means learning to communicate better using new methods. He felt that instead of his usual approach of taking part in discussions in private, at which he excelled, he needed something new. There wasn't enough time at his disposal to hold so many one-on-one meetings. However, his struggle was that he had serious reservations about using methods, processes, and tools he had never tested.

Hans is a very pleasant person. He's a proponent of the art of paying attention, and he willingly spends extra time doing so. For example, he was the only client who called me instead of emailing to ask if we could postpone a session. On the surface, it might seem that because Hans functioned so well using personal contact, he had neglected more modern communication forms. However, he was running on an old autopilot that created uneasiness in him if he adopted new techniques, like videoconferencing or speaking from a stage. This prevented him from adopting new methods—until we located and deleted the old program.

After a structured analysis of Hans's behavior, thoughts, and ingrained priorities, we uncovered the reason he felt uncomfortable, uneasy, and hijacked when, for example, he had to speak in front of a camera. In his first job as a manager, he had received extensive training in the field of safety. The factory he was in charge of could literally blow the whole country to smithereens if it didn't follow protocol down to the slightest detail. There was no room for experimenting with new methods. In that context, it was simply not worth the risk. It could be too hazardous.

However, the context had changed. This realization didn't enter Hans's brain until we brought his autopilot into the open. After that, we could work effectively to help him use new methods to reach a larger audience and become more conspicuous to his employees. After we righted Hans's programming, it took no more than two months before he felt natural communicating with his entire organization using newer methods.

As long you are motivated, as Hans was, you can develop yourself throughout your life. The brain is in fact neuroplastic. You can continually develop new synapses, or neural connections. The more you train your brain to create new synapses, the better it becomes at doing so.

Think of forming synapses in the brain like walking through tall grass in the wild. If you walk in the same place repeatedly, a trail forms. If you leave it, the grass will stand back up, and what could have been a new trail will go back to being tall grass. It works the same way with forming new synapses. Synapses are new connections between brain cells, and the more you use them, the stronger they get. In the end, they become a new autopilot.

The first step is to be curious, observing yourself and staying open to others' observations about your behavior. Here you can discover the mental autopilots that hijack your brain because they don't fit into the situation. Coaching is a good tool for reexamining your beliefs about the world and identifying your autopilots. You can also contribute to the process on your own by questioning your beliefs, tendencies, and blind spots. We all have them. These are some examples of how you can examine them:

· Be willing to accept there may be other forms of truth and points of view besides the ones you envisage.

· Ask others for feedback and opinions about situations you think can lead to perspectives on your behavior.

· Analyze an issue by trying to include all the possible externalities you can think of.

· Muster up the courage to examine facets of your character you would like to change.

· When you have received enough data and insight, a picture may begin to form. If this doesn't happen, then divulge your thoughts and information to someone impartial whom you can trust and ask that person to act as a sparring partner with regard to your viewpoints. This person must have nothing to gain from your development—not your partner, leader, colleague, or family member.

· In this case, data is more than numbers. It also consists of experiences, testimonies, and emotions.

Imagine how much easier it would be to collaborate, to lead and be led, if everyone had a vision and an experience of the world that was the same. But things aren't so simple. The truth is that people don't experience the world in the same way and that people, organizations, and sustainability are paradoxical. Normality prescribes that our wishes counteract our values.[52] A choice that benefits one perspective might take something away from another perspective. In short, the world is complex, and if we let ourselves be carried away by a desire to achieve simplicity, we lose sight of the nuances or details that might be the key to finding the right solution. This is where good listening skills and the concept of including externalities are vital. Do you ever interrupt when others are speaking, or draw own conclusions before you are finished listening?

When you listen to, see, and sense other people without drawing premature conclusions about how to interpret their behavior, and when you meet other people and yourself with an open mind and inquisitiveness, then you give them and yourself greater freedom to act. With this freedom, you have the chance to do what is best instead of reacting based on your autopilot.

Personal and professional development is like a journey of discovery. So much of what we do and say happens automatically, dictated by automatic programs. But as described earlier, when we become conscious of these autopilots, we can make greater progress.

NEXT-LEVEL AWARENESS

In this book, you have encountered leaders who, while working alone or with others, became hijacked and lost their energy, then built up their energy, became agile. You have received a series of tools and different perspectives that can help you do the same.

It doesn't matter whether you're a leader or not. We have freedom, influence, and a responsibility to be co-authors of what we take part in—even if the context plays a significant role. If we're smart, we can be aware of our context and be agile. In an agile state, we'll not only become more able to ensure prosperity and development for ourselves and others, but also become better at some of these challenges:

- · accepting changes
- · being innovative and creative
- · understanding and working with new technology or marketing conditions

- creating synergy in an M&A or other new collaboration
- feeling less insecure, exposed, or badly treated
- collaborating with someone we don't like
- leading more personnel than we can keep an eye on
- accepting a leader we feel uncertain about
- doing something we haven't done before
- taking part in restructuring an organization
- changing jobs
- living with unforeseeable and unknown conditions
- reducing personnel
- solving crises
- taking on greater responsibility or willingly giving up responsibility
- managing stress, either our own or that of others

I believe this is the next level of work and collaboration. Hence, the human brain hasn't developed a lot over the past 10,000 years, and we need it to. With the courage to develop yourself, you can affect the energy level at work as well as the results and relationships—and it'll never be boring. It can be an exciting adventure to begin to register your autopilots, your hasty conclusions, your bodily signals, your status as agile or hijacked, and your energy levels, as well as those of the people you're collaborating with. Just remember the experiences of Stephanie and Philip. They have truly felt the benefits of next-level mental agility, both as individuals and in their teams and departments.

Stephanie and her employees are now the best-performing department in the Nordics based on metrics such as employee turnover, work satisfaction, customer relations, and the bottom line. In Philip's case, it has meant greater empowerment for his employees. Decreasing their experience of hierarchy has increased their power to act and their willingness to confront problems and solve them successfully. This new mental state and way of working have automatically led to a higher level of innovation, including minimizing costs and boosting customer satisfaction.

In both cases, the next-level mental state in these departments has taken their collaboration to the next level. It can do the same for you and your company, and—if you allow it—it can have a positive effect on other areas of your life as well.

I invite you to use the free resources on my website Josefinecampbell.com as I am wishing for you to wake up energized every morning—ready for whatever comes next.

I would be delighted to hear from you. Please feel free to send any inquiries, reviews, or questions to **hello@josefinecampbell.com**, or to connect with me on LinkedIn. You can check my website for free resources.

REFERENCES

American Institute of Stress. (2022). *What is stress?*

American Psychological Association (APA). (2020, October). *Stress in America 2020: A national mental health crisis.*

Andersen, J. A. (2006). Leadership, personality and effectiveness. *The Journal of Socio-Economics, 35*(6), 1078–1091.

Bales, R. F. (1950). *Interaction process analysis: A method for the study of small groups.* Addison-Wesley Press.

Brown, B. (2018). *Dare to lead—Brave work. Tough conversations. Whole hearts.* Ebury Publishing.

Brown, D. (2001). Human universals and their implications. In N. Roughley (Ed.), *Being humans: Anthropological universality and particularity in transdisciplinary perspectives* (pp. 156–174). de Gruyter.

Brown, D. E. (1988). *Hierarchy, history, and human nature: The social origins of historical consciousness.* University of Arizona Press.

Campbell, J. (2020). *Er du klar eller kapret? Bliv bedre til at samarbejde, lede og blive ledet: Vol. 1* [Are You Agile or Hijacked? Be better at collaborating, lead and be led.] (1st ed.). Forlaget Zara.

Camus, A. (2015). *Sisyfos-myten* [The myth of Sisyphus]. Gyldendal (original work published in 1942).

Castells, M. (2009). *The rise of the network society* (2nd ed.). Wiley-Blackwell.

Coyle, D. (2018). *The culture code: The secrets of highly successful groups.* Bantam.

Cullen-Lester, K. L., Webster, B. D., Edwards, B. D., & Braddy, P. W. (2018). The effect of multiple negative, neutral, and positive organizational changes. *European Journal of Work and Organizational Psychology, 28*(1), 124–135.

Dattani, S., Ritchie, H., & Roser, M. (2021, August). *Mental health.* Our World in Data.

Eigel, K. M. (1998). *Leader effectiveness: A constructive-developmental view and investigation* [Doctoral dissertation, University of Georgia].

Flavia C., Moreno, V., & Hickmann, M. (2012). Effects of leader intelligence, personality and emotional intelligence on transformational leadership and managerial performance. *The Leadership Quarterly, 23,* 443–455.

Frankl, V. (2006). *Man's search for meaning* (4th ed.). Beacon Press.

Frei, F., & Morriss, A. (2020). Begin with trust: The first step to becoming a genuinely empowering leader. *Harvard Business Review, 98*(3), 112–121.

Gilbert, D. (2007). *Stumbling on happiness.* Random House.

Global Organization for Stress. *Stress facts.* Global Organization for Stress. Retrieved April 12, 2022

Goleman, D. (2017). *What makes a leader?* Harvard Business Review Press.

Harari, Y. N. (2015). *Sapiens: A brief history of humankind.* Random House.

Hart, S. (2009). *Den følsomme hjerne—hjernens udvikling gennem tilknytning og samhørighedsbånd* [The sensitive brain, the brain's development trough affiliation, and strings of interconnections]. Gyldendal.

Harter, J. (2018, August 26). *Employee engagement on the rise in the U.S.* Gallup.

Harter, J. (2020, October 16). *U.S. employee engagement reverts back to pre-COVID-19 levels.* Gallup.

Heifetz, R. A., & Laurie, D. L. (2001). The work of leadership. *Harvard Business Review, 79*(11), 131.

Herold, D. M., Fedor, D. B., & Caldwell, S. D. (2007). Beyond change management: A multilevel investigation of contextual and personal influences on employees' commitment to change. *Journal of Applied Psychology*, *92*(4), 942–951

Hull, M., (Ed.). (2021, August 18). *Mental health disorders*. The Recovery Village.

Johnson, S. (1998). *Who moved my cheese?* Putnam Adult.

Karasek, R. (1989). Krav-kontrol modellen: Dens udvikling og status [Demand-control Model: The Development and Status.]. *Arbejdspsykologisk Bulletin*, *5*, 16–35.

Kegan, R., & Lahey, L. L. (2009). *Immunity to change: How to overcome it and unlock the potential in yourself and your organization*. Harvard Business Review Press.

Kierkegaard, S. (1843). *Enten—Eller: et Livs Fragment* [Either/Or: a fragment of life]. C. A. Reitzel.

Kleitman, N. (1963). *Sleep and wakefulness*. University of Chicago Press.

Kleitman, N. (1982). Basic rest-activity cycle—22 years later. *Journal of Sleep Research & Sleep Medicine*, *5*(4), 311–317.

Krautwald, A. (2018). *Unge generationer på arbejde—Vejen til et anderledes rigt liv* [Ung Generations at Work—The Road to a Different Richter Life]. Dansk Psykologisk Forlag.

Lindeløv, J. K. (2012, September 2). *Bruger vi kun 10 procent af hjernen?* [Do we use only 10 percent of our brain?]. Videnskab.dk.

Mental Health Foundation. (2018). *Stress: Are we coping?*

Miller, E. K., & Cohen, J. D. (2001). An integrative theory of prefrontal cortex function. *Annual Review of Neuroscience, 24*(1), 167–202.

OOP & The Chartered Institute of Personnel and Development. (2008, July). *Fight, flight or face it: Celebrating the effective management of conflict.* CIPD.

Patnaik, J. B. (2011). Organizational culture: The key to effective leadership and work motivation. *Social Science International, 27*(1), 79–94.

Pencavel, J. (2014). The productivity of working hours. *Institute for the Study of Labor, 8129*, 1–54.

Plato (1998). The apology of Socrates. In T. G. West & H. S. West (Trans.), *Four texts on Socrates*, Cornell University Press (original work published ca. 399 B.C.E.).

Preston, S. D., & de Waal, F. B. M. (2002). Empathy: Its ultimate and proximate bases. *Behavioral and Brain Sciences, 25*(1), 1–20.

Rock, D. (2009). *Your brain at work—Strategies for overcoming distraction, regaining focus, and working smarter all day long.* HarperCollins Publishers.

Schein, E. H. (1985). *Organizational culture and leadership.* Jossey-Bass Publishers.

Senge, P. M. (1994). *The fifth discipline fieldbook: Strategies and tools for building a learning organization.* Currency Press.

Taylor, C. (1991). *The malaise of modernity.* House of Anansi Press.

Taylor, F. W. (1913). *The principles of scientific management.* Harper & Brothers Publishers.

World Commission on Environment and Development (WCED). (1987). *Report of the World Commission on Environment and Development: Our common future.* United Nations.

World Health Organization (WHO). (2019, October 2). *10 facts on mental health.*

World Health Organization (WHO). (2021, September 13). *Depression.*

Zuckerman, A. (2020, May 21). *61 stress statistics: 2020/2021 facts, causes & effects.* CompareCamp.

American Institute of Stress. (2022). *What is stress?*

American Psychological Association (APA). (2020, October). *Stress in America 2020: A national mental health crisis.*

Andersen, J. A. (2006). Leadership, personality and effectiveness. *The Journal of Socio-Economics, 35*(6), 1078–1091.

Bales, R. F. (1950). *Interaction process analysis: A method for the study of small groups.* Addison-Wesley Press.

Brown, B. (2018). *Dare to lead—Brave work. Tough conversations. Whole hearts.* Ebury Publishing.

Brown, D. (2001). Human universals and their implications. In N. Roughley (Ed.), *Being humans: Anthropological universality and particularity in transdisciplinary perspectives* (pp. 156–174). de Gruyter.

Brown, D. E. (1988). *Hierarchy, history, and human nature: The social origins of historical consciousness.* University of Arizona Press.

Campbell, J. (2020). *Er du klar eller kapret? Bliv bedre til at samarbejde, lede og blive ledet: Vol. 1* [Are You Agile or Hijacked? Be better at collaborating, lead and be led.] (1st ed.). Forlaget Zara.

Camus, A. (2015). *Sisyfos-myten* [The myth of Sisyphus]. Gyldendal (original work published in 1942).

Castells, M. (2009). *The rise of the network society* (2nd ed.). Wiley-Blackwell.

Coyle, D. (2018). *The culture code: The secrets of highly successful groups.* Bantam.

Cullen-Lester, K. L., Webster, B. D., Edwards, B. D., & Braddy, P. W. (2018). The effect of multiple negative, neutral, and positive organizational changes. *European Journal of Work and Organizational Psychology, 28*(1), 124–135.

Dattani, S., Ritchie, H., & Roser, M. (2021, August). *Mental health.* Our World in Data.

Eigel, K. M. (1998). *Leader effectiveness: A constructive-developmental view and investigation* [Doctoral dissertation, University of Georgia].

Flavia C., Moreno, V., & Hickmann, M. (2012). Effects of leader intelligence, personality and emotional intelligence on transformational leadership and managerial performance. *The Leadership Quarterly, 23,* 443–455.

Frankl, V. (2006). *Man's search for meaning* (4th ed.). Beacon Press.

Frei, F., & Morriss, A. (2020). Begin with trust: The first step to becoming a genuinely empowering leader. *Harvard Business Review, 98*(3), 112–121.

Gilbert, D. (2007). *Stumbling on happiness.* Random House.

Global Organization for Stress. *Stress facts.* Global Organization for Stress. Retrieved April 12, 2022

Goleman, D. (2017). *What makes a leader?* Harvard Business Review Press.

Harari, Y. N. (2015). *Sapiens: A brief history of humankind.* Random House.

Hart, S. (2009). *Den følsomme hjerne—hjernens udvikling gennem tilknytning og samhørighedsbånd* [The sensitive brain, the brain's development trough affiliation, and strings of interconnections]. Gyldendal.

Harter, J. (2018, August 26). *Employee engagement on the rise in the U.S.* Gallup.

Harter, J. (2020, October 16). *U.S. employee engagement reverts back to pre-COVID-19 levels.* Gallup.

Heifetz, R. A., & Laurie, D. L. (2001). The work of leadership. *Harvard Business Review, 79*(11), 131.

Herold, D. M., Fedor, D. B., & Caldwell, S. D. (2007). Beyond change management: A multilevel investigation of contextual and personal influences on employees' commitment to change. *Journal of Applied Psychology, 92*(4), 942–951

Hull, M., (Ed.). (2021, August 18). *Mental health disorders.* The Recovery Village.

Johnson, S. (1998). *Who moved my cheese?* Putnam Adult.

Karasek, R. (1989). Krav-kontrol modellen: Dens udvikling og status [Demand-control Model: The Development and Status.]. *Arbejdspsykologisk Bulletin, 5*, 16–35.

Kegan, R., & Lahey, L. L. (2009). *Immunity to change: How to overcome it and unlock the potential in yourself and your organization.* Harvard Business Review Press.

Kierkegaard, S. (1843). *Enten—Eller: et Livs Fragment* [Either/Or: a fragment of life]. C. A. Reitzel.

Kleitman, N. (1963). *Sleep and wakefulness.* University of Chicago Press.

Kleitman, N. (1982). Basic rest-activity cycle—22 years later. *Journal of Sleep Research & Sleep Medicine, 5*(4), 311–317.

Krautwald, A. (2018). *Unge generationer på arbejde—Vejen til et anderledes rigt liv* [Ung Generations at Work—The Road to a Different Richter Life]. Dansk Psykologisk Forlag.

Lindeløv, J. K. (2012, September 2). *Bruger vi kun 10 procent af hjernen?* [Do we use only 10 percent of our brain?]. Videnskab.dk.

Mental Health Foundation. (2018). *Stress: Are we coping?*

Miller, E. K., & Cohen, J. D. (2001). An integrative theory of prefrontal cortex function. *Annual Review of Neuroscience, 24*(1), 167–202.

OOP & The Chartered Institute of Personnel and Development. (2008, July). *Fight, flight or face it: Celebrating the effective management of conflict*. CIPD.

Patnaik, J. B. (2011). Organizational culture: The key to effective leadership and work motivation. *Social Science International, 27*(1), 79–94.

Pencavel, J. (2014). The productivity of working hours. *Institute for the Study of Labor, 8129*, 1–54.

Plato (1998). The apology of Socrates. In T. G. West & H. S. West (Trans.), *Four texts on Socrates*, Cornell University Press (original work published ca. 399 B.C.E.).

Preston, S. D., & de Waal, F. B. M. (2002). Empathy: Its ultimate and proximate bases. *Behavioral and Brain Sciences, 25*(1), 1–20.

Rock, D. (2009). *Your brain at work—Strategies for overcoming distraction, regaining focus, and working smarter all day long.* HarperCollins Publishers.

Schein, E. H. (1985). *Organizational culture and leadership.* Jossey-Bass Publishers.

Senge, P. M. (1994). *The fifth discipline fieldbook: Strategies and tools for building a learning organization.* Currency Press.

Taylor, C. (1991). *The malaise of modernity.* House of Anansi Press.

Taylor, F. W. (1913). *The principles of scientific management.* Harper & Brothers Publishers.

World Commission on Environment and Development (WCED). (1987). *Report of the World Commission on Environment and Development: Our common future.* United Nations.

World Health Organization (WHO). (2019, October 2). *10 facts on mental health.*

World Health Organization (WHO). (2021, September 13). *Depression.*

Zuckerman, A. (2020, May 21). *61 stress statistics: 2020/2021 facts, causes & effects.* CompareCamp.

ENDNOTES

CHAPTER 1

1   Lindeløv, J. K. (2012, September 2). *Bruger vi kun 10 procent af hjernen?* [Do we use only 10% of our brain?]. Videnskab.dk.

2   Taylor, C. (1991). *The malaise of modernity.* House of Anansi Press.

3   World Health Organization (WHO). (2021, September 13). *Depression.*

4   American Institute of Stress, 2022.

5   Zuckerman, A. (2020, May 21). *61 stress statistics: 2020/2021 facts, causes & effects.* CompareCamp.

6   Global Organization for Stress (2022). *Stress facts.* Global Organization for Stress. Retrieved April 12.

7   Harter, J. (2018, August 26). *Employee engagement on the rise in the U.S.* Gallup.

     Harter, J. (2020, October 16). *U.S. employee engagement reverts back to pre-COVID-19 levels.* Gallup.

8   American Psychological Association (APA). (2020, October). *Stress in America 2020: A national mental health crisis.*

9   Mental Health Foundation. (2018). *Stress: Are we coping?*

10 Bales, R. F. (1950). Interaction process analysis: A method for the study of small groups. Addison-Wesley Press.

11 Bales was a professor of social relations and director of the Laboratory of Social Relations at Harvard University. He pioneered the development of systematic methods for group observation and measurement of interaction processes. His first coding system was Interactive Process Analysis (IPA), which was used to classify group behavior as task-oriented or relationship-oriented. In this method, a group is observed and its members' interactions are classified. Bales classified being formal along with being passive, showing disagreement, and failing to help. So, Bales judged formal behavior as damaging to group dynamics. Read more in Bales (1950).

12 Gilbert, D. (2007). *Stumbling on happiness.* Random House.

CHAPTER 2

13 Cullen-Lester, K. L., Webster, B. D., Edwards, B. D., & Braddy, P. W. (2018). The effect of multiple negative, neutral, and positive organizational changes. *European Journal of Work and Organizational Psychology, 28*(1), 124–135.

14 Coyle, D. (2018). *The culture code: The secrets of highly successful groups.* Bantam

CHAPTER 3

15   Lindeløv, J. K. (2012, September 2). *Bruger vi kun 10 procent af hjernen?* [Do we use only 10% of our brain?]. Videnskab.dk.

16   Pencavel, J. (2014). The productivity of working hours. *Institute for the Study of Labor, 8129*, 1–54.

17   Kleitman, N. (1963). *Sleep and wakefulness.* University of Chicago Press

18   Rock, D. (2009). Your brain at work—Strategies for overcoming distraction, regaining focus, and working smarter all day long. HarperCollins Publishers.

19   OOP & The Chartered Institute of Personnel and Development. (2008, July). *Fight, flight or face it: Celebrating the effective management of conflict.* CIPD.

20   World Health Organization (WHO). (2019, October 2). *10 facts on mental health.*

CHAPTER 4

21   Kierkegaard, S. (1843). *Enten—Eller: et Livs Fragment* [Either/Or: a fragment of life]. C. A. Reitzel.

22   Plato (1998). The apology of Socrates. In T. G. West & H. S. West (Trans.), *Four texts on Socrates,* Cornell University Press (original work published ca. 399 B.C.E.).

23   Hart, S. (2009). Den følsomme hjerne—hjernens udvikling gennem tilknytning og samhørighedsbånd [The sensitive brain, the brain's development trough affiliation, and strings of interconnections]. Gyldendal.

24   The prefrontal cortex (PFC) is the front part of the brain's frontal lobe. It controls our planning of complex cognitive behavior, personal expressions, decision-making, and social behavior. See Miller, E. K., & Cohen, J. D. (2001). An integrative theory of prefrontal cortex function. *Annual Review of Neuroscience, 24*(1), 167–202.

25   Rock, D. (2009). *Your brain at work—Strategies for overcoming distraction, regaining focus, and working smarter all day long.* HarperCollins Publishers.

26   The sandwich principle is about layering criticism or constructive feedback between two instances of positive feedback or praise, like meat between two slices of bread. This technique is used even when only wanting to give criticism or constructive feedback and requires the giver to think of two positive things to say about the receiver.

CHAPTER 5

27   Robert Karasek—a sociologist from the US— developed the demand-control model in 1989. It has become one of the best-known models with regard to workload and work-related stress. This model is key to Philip's management methodology.

Karasek, R. (1989). Krav-kontrol modellen: Dens udvikling òg status [Demand-control Model: The Development and Status.]. Arbejdspsykologisk Bulletin, 5, 16–35.

CHAPTER 6

28   Kegan, R., & Lahey, L. L. (2009). Immunity to change: How to overcome it and unlock the potential in yourself and your organization. Harvard Business Review Press.

29 Rock, D. (2009). *Your brain at work—Strategies for overcoming distraction, regaining focus, and working smarter all day long.* HarperCollins Publishers.

30 Herold, D. M., Fedor, D. B., & Caldwell, S. D. (2007). Beyond change management: A multilevel investigation of contextual and personal influences on employees' commitment to change. *Journal of Applied Psychology, 92*(4), 942–951.

31 American Psychological Association (APA). (2020, October). *Stress in America 2020: A national mental health crisis.*

32 Heifetz, R. A., & Laurie, D. L. (2001). The work of leadership. Harvard Business Review, 79(11), 131.

33 Kegan, R., & Lahey, L. L. (2009). Immunity to change: How to overcome it and unlock the potential in yourself and your organization. Harvard Business Review Press.

34 Heifetz, R. A., & Laurie, D. L. (2001). The work of leadership. Harvard Business Review, 79(11), 131.

35 Patnaik, J. B. (2011). Organizational culture: The key to effective leadership and work motivation. *Social Science International, 27*(1), 79–94.

36 A few of the studies showing this are Andersen, 2006; Eigel, 1998; Flavia et al., 2012; Goleman, 1998; and Heifetz, R. A., & Laurie, D. L. (2001). The work of leadership. Harvard Business Review, 79(11), 131.

37 Peter Drucker is described as the founder of modern management. The first notion we have of this quote from him is in Schein (1985), p. 33. However, the exact date he made the statement is unknown. Schein, E. H. (1985). Organizational culture and leadership. Jossey-Bass Publishers. P. 33.

38 Brown, D. (2001). Human universals and their implications. In N. Roughley (Ed.), Being humans: Anthropological universality and particularity in transdisciplinary perspectives (pp. 156–174). de Gruyter.
And; Brown, D. E. (1988). Hierarchy, history, and human nature: The social origins of historical consciousness. University of Arizona Press.

39 Kegan, R., & Lahey, L. L. (2009). Immunity to change: How to overcome it and unlock the potential in yourself and your organization. Harvard Business Review Press.

40 Frei, F., & Morriss, A. (2020). Begin with trust: The first step to becoming a genuinely empowering leader. *Harvard Business Review, 98*(3), 112–121.

41 Kegan and Lahey (2009) developed the SAFE test method. I use it with great resonance in my coaching practice to secure the development of my coachees. Kegan, R., & Lahey, L. L. (2009). Immunity to change: How to overcome it and unlock the potential in yourself and your organization. Harvard Business Review Press.

CHAPTER 7

42 Rock, D. (2009). *Your brain at work—Strategies for overcoming distraction, regaining focus, and working smarter all day long.* HarperCollins Publishers.

43 OOP & The Chartered Institute of Personnel and Development. (2008, July). *Fight, flight or face it: Celebrating the effective management of conflict.* CIPD.

44   Homer is not a historian by the modern definition. His work would not pass as scientific today. But as he and Herodotus are some of the first storytellers whose tales survived and were written down early on, they are used as historical sources regarding ancient Greek history.

45   Camus, A. (2015). Sisyfos-myten [The myth of Sisyphus]. Gyldendal (original work published in 1942).

46   Frankl, V. (2006). *Man's search for meaning* (4th ed.). Beacon Press.

47   Frankl, V. (2006). *Man's search for meaning* (4th ed.). Beacon Press.

48   Frankl, V. (2006). *Man's search for meaning* (4th ed.). Beacon Press.

49   Johnson, S. (1998). *Who moved my cheese?* Putnam Adult.

50   Herold, D. M., Fedor, D. B., & Caldwell, S. D. (2007). Beyond change management: A multilevel investigation of contextual and personal influences on employees' commitment to change. *Journal of Applied Psychology, 92*(4), 942–951.

51   Senge, P. M. (1994). The fifth discipline fieldbook: Strategies and tools for building a learning organization. Currency Press.

52   Brown, B. (2018). Dare to lead—Brave work. Tough conversations. Whole hearts. Ebury Publishing.

ABOUT THE AUTHOR

 **JOSEFINE CAMPBELL** is an author and an Executive Coach with expertise in leadership. Her clientele includes large multinational companies such as Maersk, Novo Nordisk, McDonald's, Carlsberg and Deloitte among others.

Prior to founding her consulting company, Josefine was an external lecturer at Copenhagen Business School and quadrable Danish Champion in Jiu jitsu.

Josefine has earned praise from her Executive Coaching clients for how easily her techniques are adapted and used by the leaders and other professionals when they have to deal with challenges at work. She emphasizes, "Being agile as a mental stage is not exclusive for martial art champions. It doesn't depend on your gender, race, size or any other outer characteristic. It is accessible to anyone."